DODGE

Boats

ANTHONY S. MOLLICA JR.

MBI

Dedication

To Mary, Margaret, and Tony,
who understand the importance of strong family values
and the quiet satisfaction of achieving worthy goals

● ●

This edition first published in 2003 by Motorbooks International, an imprint of MBI Publishing Company, Galtier Plaza, Suite 200, 380 Jackson Street, St. Paul, MN 55101-3885 USA

Motorbooks International titles are also available at discounts in bulk quantity for industrial or sales-promotional use. For details write to Special Sales Manager at Motorbooks International Wholesalers & Distributors, Galtier Plaza, Suite 200, 380 Jackson Street, St. Paul, MN 55101-3885 USA.

Library of Congress Cataloging-in-Publication Data

Mollica, Anthony S., 1932-
   Dodge boats / by Anthony Mollica, Jr.
    p. cm.
   ISBN 0-7603-1174-9 (hc. : alk. paper)
    1. Motorboats--United States--History--
   20th century. 2. Chrysler Corporation.
   Dodge Division--History--20th century. I. Title.

VM341.M64985 2003
623.8'231'0973--dc21

Front cover: Elgin, the superb 21-foot, 1931 Dodge split-cockpit runabout, demonstrates its modern lines and abundant flare while splitting the waves on Lake Tahoe. *Robert Bruce Duncan*

Frontispiece: When the 20-foot, 1928 Sport-A-Bout met with slower public acceptance than Horace Dodge Jr. had anticipated, it was restyled as a more convetional runabout featuring a varnished hull and traditional Dodge trim. The result was a more appealing model. *Marty Loken*

Title pages: Ninety 16-foot, 1930 Dodge Runabouts, varnished and nearly finished, await engine installation, upholstery, and deck hardware in an area of the Newport News, Virginia, factory filled with superb natural lighting.

Back cover: (Top) The center-mounted nautical wheel in the 1935, 16-foot Standard Utility identified as the "Fishing Boat" used a pulley system to help keep the cost under $500. *Gary Michael (Bottom left)* Horace III and Delphine, children from Horace Dodge Jr.'s first marriage to Lois Knowlson, join their father aboard ship to sail to his residence in England in 1935. *(Bottom right)* In 1929, Horace Jr. reached back to his automotive roots and commissioned the respected commercial artist Edward A. Wilson to create a series of print ads for Dodge boats. The 30 paintings that resulted helped reestablish Dodge as an important force in the boating industry.

Edited by Dennis Pernu and Joe Cabadas
Designed by LeAnn Kuhlmann

Printed in China

CONTENTS

PREFACE

• •

An undeniable reward of researching the past is the rediscovery of personal events in a new context. My fondness for boats and the pleasures of boating is a natural part of my life that hasn't diminished or overpowered my other interests. In recalling the events that expanded my interest in boats, I vividly remember the first time I saw a big mahogany runabout in the summer of 1939. I was seven years old and visiting the Syracuse Yacht Club on Oneida Lake when I spotted a very large, sleek runabout at one of the docks. It had three separate cockpits for passengers. I looked at the cockpit that was all the way in the back of the boat and thought, *This would be a wonderful place sit while going for a ride.*

The word "Fore" was painted in very large letters on each side of the hull. Its meaning puzzled me. When I asked my older brother about it, he said that "Fore" was the boat's name. Then I asked him what it meant. He told me that it was a term shouted by golfers to warn other golfers to take cover or watch out because a golf ball was headed their way. I imagined this huge boat traveling at high speed with the big "Fore" on the hull warning other boaters to get out of its way. I thought to myself, *What a great name for this boat.*

Then I spotted a rubber step pad and I saw the words "Dodge Watercar" in raised letters. I asked my brother, "What's a Watercar?" His terse reply was "It's a boat!" It was clear from his response that I had just asked him my last question regarding this big boat. For several years I looked forward to seeing *Fore* each summer as it sped out of our harbor with loads of joyful passengers. And then, one summer, it was gone. I never saw *Fore* again.

When I was 15, I attended Manlius Military Academy in upstate New York. At my new school I spent many hours playing basketball in a building known as the Dodge Gymnasium. It took nearly two years before I made the connection with the name on the outside of the school gymnasium and the Dodges that manufactured automobiles and the Watercar boats. I was in the school library when my curiosity resulted in a little research to see if there was a connection among the gym, the cars, and the boats.

With a bit of help from the librarian, I learned that Horace Dodge Sr., builder of the Dodge automobile, had provided the funds for the school's Dodge Gymnasium. I also learned that his son, Horace Dodge Jr., had attended my school 25 years before and was the person responsible for building the Watercar runabouts. This was an interesting discovery and made me appreciate the importance of libraries in my life, a lesson that proved to be valuable years later for the development of this book.

The information I learned made me feel as if Dodge and I were linked in some way. From that moment forward, I held a very special appreciation for the Dodges, their wonderful boats, and their gift of the gymnasium where I played basketball and dreamed of being a star. Horace Dodge Jr. became a special celebrity to me.

More than 60 years have passed since my first glimpse of the wonderful Watercar named *Fore*, but my enthusiasm for Dodge boats never diminished. Each time I have had a chance to ride in one, I took advantage of the opportunity.

Horace Dodge Jr.'s desire to bring the cost of boating within reach of the average family, just as his own father and uncle had accomplished with Dodge automobiles, was a challenging and worthy goal. He contributed important ideas and a new vitality that influenced the entire stodgy boat-building industry. Yet in spite of his remarkable achievements, little recognition has been attributed to his leading influence during the classic boating era.

— *Anthony S. Mollica Jr.*

ACKNOWLEDGMENTS

One of the most rewarding aspects of undertaking research into a lesser-known topic is the generous cooperation often received from so many interested people. There were many obstacles preparing this illustrated history of Dodge boats. It was clear from the beginning that fulfillment could be achieved only through the assistance and interest of additional contributors.

Dodge was one of the important boat builders and innovators of the classic runabout era, but nearly every bit of information that exists of its operations seems scattered in many small private collections. Indeed, I have been fortunate in my quest for facts and photographs that interested Dodge enthusiasts became just as excited about seeing this book completed as the author. Only with the help of many people could this book be prepared and completed.

I want to acknowledge my sincere appreciation to each of the following contributors for their enduring generosity and assistance in this work: Russ Arrand, Chris Byrnes, William T. Campbell, Edwin Dodge, James Domm, John Dubickas, Curt Erickson, Frank Fierro Jr., Thomas Frauenheim, Rebecca Hopfinger, Lindsey Hopkins, Spencer Jenkins, William King, Paul Kleppert, Charles LeFebvre, Martin Lokin, Gary Michael, William Miller, Tom Mittler, Robert Moharter, Harold Orchard, Scott Ouderkirk, Scott Peters, Patricia Rich, Darlene Sargent, Jeffrey Stebbins, Spike Steele, Al Schinnerer, Robert Schroeder, F. Todd Warner, Robert Weaver, and Mary Whittell.

INTRODUCTION

The story of the Dodge brothers, John and Horace Sr., is one of the most fascinating in the development of American industry. They used their extraordinary skill and work ethic to build components for the Model T, rated by many historians as *the* car of the twentieth century. Plus, they launched their own popular car in 1914. Horace Dodge Jr. brought this same creative spirit to building popular boats. His vision for revolutionizing boat building was every bit as creative as the Dodge brothers' was to the auto industry.

The story of Dodge boats began with the legacy of the Dodge brothers, whose incredible rise to prominence in Detroit provided young Horace with a superb model of industrial success and the means to establish himself quickly. The rapid development of the internal combustion engine was essential to the growth of both the American auto and pleasure-boat industries, which were intertwined in the early days.

Early on, auto manufacturers tested the endurance of their engines by running them in boats at high speeds and under strenuous conditions. Boat racing thus became, and remains today, a popular and effective way to assess automobile engine designs while providing information for future improvements.

In 1904 the American Power Boat Challenge Cup Regatta was established. It was a watershed event in the boating industry, attracting a strong following among boating enthusiasts and the media. The winning boat owner took home the Gold Cup trophy and had the privilege of defending the title at his yacht club the following year. More powerful engines and new designs followed quickly.

As engines became reliable and more powerful, designers became far more creative too. Design changes, in turn, fueled an eager appetite by excited buyers for frequent improvements. Young entrepreneurs also could enter the industry.

When Horace Dodge Jr. was 16, Chris Smith of Algonac, Michigan, was commissioned by a prominent group of Detroit industrialists to build a race boat that could win the Gold Cup. Horace Jr.'s father and uncle were enthusiastic yachtsmen and supported the effort to end the eastern yacht clubs' dominance of the race. *Miss Detroit* was a beautiful, fast race boat that won the 1916 Gold Cup and brought the trophy to the Motor City for the first time. Young Horace Dodge was captivated by the victory and pledged that someday soon he would win the Gold Cup with his own race boat.

Horace Jr. entered the boat-building scene during, arguably, its most exciting period. Powerboat racing was a new and fascinating sport that attracted huge gatherings of spectators.

In 1920 American Gold Cup champion Gar Wood shipped his superb race boats to England to challenge for the coveted Harmsworth Trophy, which was emblematic of the world's fastest boats. He won the race convincingly, and upon returning to America, scores of buyers ordered Gar Wood boats.

Chris Smith and his dedicated sons decided to end their six-year partnership with Gar Wood and once again establish their own boat-building operation. It was a courageous move that met with remarkable success under the banner Chris-Craft. Detroit's John Hacker and New York's George Crouch also designed and built innovative, exotic speedboats destined to become cherished objects of art in the years ahead. It was a time of extraordinary achievements for boating enthusiasts. Young Horace believed that he could be a bigger player as a boat builder than as an automaker and yearned to bring the lessons his family had learned making cars to the manufacture of boats.

In 1920 John and Horace Sr. suddenly became seriously ill and died within a year of each other. The two surviving Dodge families were left with an enormous fortune and control of one of America's most promising and successful industrial operations. Although their wealth was assured, the two Dodge widows were thrust into demanding new roles that would challenge them for the rest of their lives.

Horace Jr. stepped away from the golden opportunity to enter the automobile business, preferring instead to establish himself as a builder of motorboats and a successful boat racer. An astonishingly confident 23-year-old Horace Jr. was eager to follow and, ultimately, planned to exceed the achievements of his idol, Gar Wood. From Dodge's viewpoint, he possessed the wealth, the motivation, and the youth to surpass Wood's daunting accomplishments.

To exceed all that Gar Wood had achieved, however, was an ambitious goal. Wood's success was legendary as an inventor, an entrepreneur, a successful boat builder, and a racing champion of international prominence. Yet Dodge was determined to supplant Gar Wood's success and become Detroit's next rising star. With the assurance of great family wealth behind him, this lofty goal became his life's ambition.

Chapter One

The Dodge Brothers Seek Their Fortune

John and Horace Dodge were born in Niles, a town in southwestern Michigan, just north of South Bend, Indiana; John Francis was born in 1864 and Horace Elgin four years later. Both boys had fiery red hair and personalities to match. Their father, Daniel, was a self-taught machinist of modest skill who operated a small shop on the edge of the St. Joseph River. Daniel involved both of his sons in the family trade while they were still in their boyhood.

The Dodge boys demonstrated an unusual aptitude for precision work in their father's shop and enjoyed working long hours to develop different solutions to knotty problems. It wasn't long before the brothers earned a reputation for their fine work and creative problem-solving skills. But Niles was a very small community and the Dodges often struggled to find enough work to support their family. Years later John described his and Horace's early childhood by saying, "We were the poorest little urchins ever born."

John also recalled with great respect their mother Maria's religious principles, noting, "[O]nce each week we were dressed like little gentlemen for Sunday school" at their Methodist church. It was also Maria who ensured that the brothers' attendance at school was always perfect.

The Dodge brothers' diligence in their father's shop, their religious upbringing, and their compulsory school attendance would prove vital in their future achievements. Both boys, however, were quick-tempered and always ready for a fight when it was required. Horace was very sensitive about his name and preferred to be called Elgin during his school days.

By 1886 John and Horace realized that prospects for marketing their skills looked much more promising in Michigan's growing community of Battle Creek. Now 22 and 18 years old, the brothers convinced their father that it would be prudent for the whole family to leave Niles for the chance to achieve greater prosperity. However, they quickly realized that the opportunities in Battle Creek weren't what they had hoped for. Without a great deal of hesitation, they moved on to Port Huron, Michigan, on the St. Clair River, a gateway city to Detroit.

With the abundance of ships and a shipbuilding industry in Port Huron, the Dodges were sure that their experience in Niles repairing marine steam engines would present a multitude of openings. This time, however, they lacked the capital to purchase the expensive tools they needed to compete against the established service operators. When they couldn't obtain marine work regularly, John and Horace often resorted to repairing agricultural machines.

Once again it became apparent that they needed to move on, this time to Detroit. With a population exceeding 100,000 residents, Detroit had an abundance of foundries and machine shops. It was only 60 miles away and offered all the opportunity and excitement of a big city. John used his well-developed bravado and appealing personality to convince employers that both he and his younger brother could deliver the quality and quantity of work required. John was always confident that his highly skilled and resourceful younger brother possessed the talent to make good on any promises that he made to impress a potential employer.

The Brothers Pay Their Dues

In late 1886 Tom Murphy, a marine engineer and owner of the Murphy Boiler Works, hired John and Horace for $18 a week to build and repair their huge cast-iron boilers. The husky, rugged Dodge brothers were well prepared for the hot, strenuous, and challenging work. With the security of regular paychecks from the Murphy Boiler Works and their father's additional monetary contributions, the Dodge family was able to enjoy a comfortable, albeit modest, living in their newly adopted big city less than a year after leaving Niles.

For a lengthy period of time, John had to give up the strenuous work at Murphy's Boiler Works after he developed a persistent, hacking cough that often left him weak and required bed rest for long periods. It was never clearly diagnosed but was later believed to be the early signs of tuberculosis. Although John completely recovered, he was eventually forced to quit Murphy's, and Horace took on an extra job at Leland & Faulconer, a precision machine shop in Detroit, to help pay John's bills. The exacting tolerances required on the job by proprietor Henry Leland presented a wonderful opportunity for Horace to demonstrate skills that contrasted to the brute force required at Murphy's. Horace enjoyed the work at Leland & Faulconer's so much that he and John decided to search for positions that encouraged the development of precise skills rather than arduous physical labor.

After six years at Murphy's Boiler Works, Horace began his search for a better opportunity for himself and John. The Dominion Typography Company in Windsor, Ontario, just across the Detroit River, seemed to be what they were seeking. When they were told that only one staff position was open, John insisted that the brothers always worked together and that if Dominion didn't have room for both, then neither would accept the position. His gambit succeeded and both were hired, each receiving salaries of $150 a month to work with micrometers and calipers. To the delight of their new employers, the brothers excelled. Then, as demand for typographers slowed down, the company began making bicycles.

In 1892 John married a Canadian-born dressmaker, Ivy Hawkins, who was earning her own living as a highly successful seamstress. John purchased a small home of his own in the same neighborhood where his parents and Horace lived. The marriage brought many changes to

John's life, but his close relationship to Horace remained solid. By 1898 the new couple had three children: Winifred, Isabel, and John Duval.

It was also at about this time that Horace began courting Christina O. Thompson, an accomplished pianist and violinist born in Scotland. Her father was a sailmaker and she contributed to the family income by providing piano lessons. Horace and Christina were married in 1896 and moved into the family home with his parents. Just a year later, Daniel Dodge died at the age of 79. He lived long enough to see all his children settled and the prospects of their comfortable future on the horizon. Two years later Horace's wife, now calling herself "Anna," gave birth to their first child, daughter Delphine. A year and a half later, their son, Horace Elgin Dodge Jr., was born on August 2, 1900.

A Business of Their Own

Bicycles were a common mode of travel for Detroit's workingmen. But the dust and grit from the city's unpaved streets wore out their parts. After long commutes, Horace found that his bike always seemed to need repairs. Part of the problem, he discovered, was that the ball bearings became clogged with fine dirt particles, so he designed a sealed housing in his home shop that resisted the invasive dust. Horace showed a working model to his brother, and John immediately saw the value of the design and knew it was a product that they could manufacture themselves.

In 1897 the Evans and Dodge Bicycle Company was founded on premises leased from Dominion Typography. Their listed partner was Fred Evans of Windsor, an investor who provided the financial backing for the Dodge brothers' enterprise. Their bicycles were designed to provide reliable, trouble-free transportation at an affordable price for workingmen like themselves. After two successful years, the Dodges and Evans sold their small but growing business to the National Cycle and Automobile Company. The new owners agreed to continue using the patented Dodge ball bearing case on their line of bicycles and to make royalty payments directly to the Dodges for each one used. National Cycle also offered to employ Horace at its Windsor plant and John at its

Hamilton, Ontario, plant. It was a very attractive offer for the Dodges, though accepting their new positions meant the brothers would be separated for the first time.

A year and a half after John moved his family to Hamilton, another firm, Canadian Cycle and Motor Company, purchased National Cycle and Automobile. Again, the new owners agreed to use Horace's ball bearing case and pay royalties for each one installed on their bicycles. In addition, the Dodge brothers negotiated a separation package with Canadian Cycle that provided each a payment of $7,500 cash. The brothers were ready to return to Detroit with enough financing to establish their own business in 1901 just as the automotive industry started to emerge.

With their combined funds from the Canadian bicycle ventures, the Dodge brothers found a location in the heart of Detroit's industrial district and, naturally, named their company "Dodge Brothers." Fifteen years had passed since they had ventured from Niles. John and Horace worked long hours creating a business that rapidly became well recognized for creative solutions, attention to details, prompt deliveries, and fair prices. It was their own enterprise and they looked forward to exceeding their customers' expectations with impeccable quality. Their new business was, indeed, becoming a labor of love, and destiny soon intervened.

Catching a Rising Star

On March 9, 1901, a devastating fire swept through the Detroit factory of pioneer automotive manufacturer Ransom E. Olds. Competition in the fledgling auto industry was so fierce that it was essential for Olds to return to production quickly before his potential customers were lost to other manufacturers. So Olds subcontracted work to suppliers for various components. The Dodges' former employer, Leland & Faulconer, received the Olds engine contract but did not have the capacity to produce engines fast enough for Olds' production volume. They recommended that Olds offer Dodge Brothers a trial engine order to see if they were up to the task. Ransom Olds knew that the Dodges were well regarded but was unsure they could meet his needs.

Necessity forced Ransom Olds to take a risk, and he awarded a modest contract to the Dodges. The brothers responded by delivering the entire order within the agreed-upon time frame. Olds was impressed with their promptness and even more excited with their flawless quality. Quickly realizing that he had located a superb subcontractor, Olds gave the Dodge Brothers additional orders, and each time they delivered the entire order as specified. Ransom Olds, in turn, was able to deliver finished cars to his customers even as he rebuilt his factory in Lansing, Michigan. His experience with the Dodges was so positive that Olds continued to use them. Suddenly, the Dodges were a regular supplier to one of Detroit's major automobile manufacturers.

In early 1902 Olds placed an order with Dodge Brothers for 3,000 transmissions. At the time, it was the largest order of its type in the auto industry and posed a severe test of Dodge Brothers' capacity to meet high-volume production. By accepting the order, the Dodges needed much larger production facilities and additional machinery, yet John and Horace were confident of their ability to expand and, at the same time, deliver finished products as promised.

The brothers acquired land to build a modern and efficient machine shop with room for future expansion. The Olds transmission order transformed the Dodge Brothers from a modest machine shop into one of the largest suppliers in the automotive industry. The most important factor in their success was their ability to do whatever was required to fulfill their contracts as promised with exceptional standards of quality. The reward for the Dodge brothers' diligence in delivering transmissions to Olds was a new level of financial achievement that instantly exceeded their modest expectations. Olds gained a major piece of the automobile market, and every Oldsmobile was delivered with a Dodge Brothers transmission. The flow of revenue allowed the brothers to explore exciting new possibilities.

Sensing the awesome potential of the automotive business and their ability to capitalize on its growth, John and Horace reinvested their profits into even bigger facilities and production improvements. The brothers took pleasure in continuously improving their products and creating more efficient production methods. The extended hours that they spent at their factory were stimulating and fulfilling to the remarkable, industrious men.

Rescuing the Dreams of Henry Ford

At nearly the same time as the Dodge Brothers grew, Henry Ford was venturing into the auto industry as the chief engineer and a minority owner of the Detroit Automobile Company. Ford had designed a prototype vehicle, but it never made it into production due to his seemingly endless procrastination. After more than a year of constant delays, the company was dissolved. Despite this setback, Ford believed if he built a successful race car, he could attract financial investors to continue in the auto business.

On October 10, 1901, Ford entered his car, *Sweepstakes*, in a race at Grosse Pointe, Michigan, against the renowned driver Alexander Winton. Surprisingly, Ford won, wooing back his old investors and attracting new ones. In 1902 the Henry Ford Company was formed but dissolved just a few months later following an argument between Ford and his backers. In 1903 he formed the Ford Motor Company, largely on the laurels of his 1901 race victory.

Ford shared his ideas for Ford Motor Company with dozens of potential backers and automobile manufacturers. When he approached the Dodge brothers to build parts for his new automobile, his accomplishments were little more than dreams. By contrast, the Dodge brothers employed more than 150 workers in a modern factory and operated without any debt. They had achieved unprecedented success and enjoyed the reward of loyal customer support.

There was no logical reason that John and Horace should entertain any notion of working with Ford, who was considered a high risk among Detroit investors. However, the Dodge brothers were intrigued by Ford's ideas and respected the associates whom Ford attracted to support his plans. Ford also offered them contractual arrangements so very favorable that they were willing to accept any risk that might be involved. It would require the full output of the Dodge factory working full shifts to meet Ford's production commitment, but if the venture was successful, they stood to gain much more than they would with the standard production arrangements of their regular clients. John and Horace also believed that they could keep Henry Ford in line if he began to falter on his commitments.

To the surprise of many, the Dodge brothers agreed to back Ford and to supply major compo-nents for his new automobile. As soon as the contract was signed, the Dodges prepared to ramp up production by purchasing new machines and specialized tools. The first payment from Ford for $5,000 was scheduled for March 15, 1903. When Ford could not make the payment because he had no outside investors and no car orders, John Dodge was unbending and told Ford that Dodge Brothers would sell every Ford part they had manufactured to other automakers if payment was not received immedi-ately. The ultimatum forced one of Ford's finan-cial backers to come up with the cash to make the payment as well as the next.

When the Ford situation did not improve, the Dodges were faced with a major decision. They could accept the fact that they had made a poor decision and lose their $50,000 investment in the venture, or they could continue to support the project by becoming investors in Ford Motor Company. They chose to invest an additional $10,000 in exchange for shares of Ford stock and became part of the Ford legend. At that time, however, the future was cloudy—if Ford fell flat, even the successful Dodge Brothers business could be strapped for cash.

The Ford Gamble Pays Off

It was recorded that a dentist from Chicago purchased the first Ford Model A on July 15, 1903. Nine months later, all 650 units for which the Dodges agreed to supply parts were sold. The following year, it was anticipated that production of Dodge running gear units needed to be increased to 750 with an option of producing 500 additional units. As it turned out, the additional components were indeed needed to meet Ford's growing demand. By March 1904, Ford Motor Company contracted and paid Dodge Brothers $162,500. In addition to an excellent profit margin, the Dodges received Ford stock dividends equal to their entire initial investment.

The Dodge brothers' gamble with Henry Ford was paying off. It wasn't just a case of good luck; the Dodges didn't place a lot of faith in luck. They backed Ford, but more importantly, they forced Ford Motor Company to fulfill every promise they said they would. It was their insistence that Ford meet his obligations that resulted in Ford's success.

Ford was considered a dreamer and a person who never made good on promises to his backers. The Dodges were virtually the only automobile investors in all of Detroit who were willing to support Ford's third entry into the auto business, and they also were tough enough to force Ford to do all that he agreed to do. It was their faith in Ford's ideas, not Ford himself, that made their involvement worth the risk.

The influence of the Dodge brothers and coal dealer Alexander Malcolmson, Ford's other major backer, gave Henry Ford his first taste of financial success. Although he held about 25 percent of the company's stock, because Henry Ford had no capital, his total investments in the project were limited to his design contributions, his patents, and his persuasive style. As Ford Motor Company succeeded, Ford was able to purchase his first suit and have a formal photograph taken by a professional photographer to capture his new image permanently.

Enjoying the Fruit of Success

The Dodge brothers continued to reinvest profits earned from Ford Motor Company into Dodge Brothers in order to be fully prepared to supply larger quantities of running gear to Ford as their anticipated increased production would require. Horace Dodge purchased a new home in a more prosperous Detroit neighborhood, selecting a two-and-a-half-story house of red brick with four bedrooms that was originally built for a Detroit lawyer 15 years earlier. Shortly after moving in, Horace added a substantial red-brick carriage house to match the architecture of the home. The new carriage house served as a workshop in which to continue to create new solutions for Dodge Brothers products. Working in his shop at home became a rewarding way to wind down a typical busy day at the factory.

John and Horace Dodge also continued to enjoy working together and even spending much of their leisure time away from the factory together, hunting, boating, and stopping off at local saloons on their way home after a long day at work. They did everything with gusto, including drinking. It was not uncommon for the talented, hard-working brothers to engage in barroom brawls. If their activities resulted in damage to the establishment, the Dodges were always there the next day to apologize and pay for the results of their roughhousing.

In 1905, when Ford Motor Company was turning out 25 cars a day and nearly 400 automo-biles each month, the majority of the component production was still being contracted to Dodge Brothers, where employment increased to nearly 300 men. Ford Motor Company was operating primarily as an assembly plant with all the necessary component units manufactured by other contractors and delivered to Ford's facility, where employees pieced together the vehicles. The more complex and more time-consuming work still required highly skilled technicians such as the Dodge brothers and their employees. The increasing need to supply components was profitable but created a great deal of pressure for Dodge Brothers and their employees.

Ford Aims for Total Control

Once Henry Ford achieved financial success, his peculiar management style emerged, revealing a total absence of loyalty to those who took great risks to help him. As investors, the Dodges sat on the Board of Directors of Ford Motor Company, but Ford gradually realized that it would be in his best interest to manufacture his own components and thus reduce his need for suppliers such as Dodge.

Ford also was determined to have total control of the company. To accomplish this, he initiated a systematic plot, with very little finesse, to push aside his loyal partner, Malcolmson. Once Ford's control was absolute, he would be able to run the company as he wished. By 1906 Dodge Brothers was supplying Ford with only axles and transmissions and once again produced components for other automobile manufacturers.

The Model T Ford, introduced in 1908, became one of the greatest success stories in automotive history, launching a revolution that would change the country and the world. Ford called his creation "the car for the great multitude." During the decade that followed, more than half of the automobiles on the road in America would be Model Ts. They were rugged, dependable cars, easy to repair, and attractively priced at $825. The wide acceptance of the Model T also was good news for the Dodges. As stockholders, they shared in Ford's profits, and as suppliers, it meant increased component sales to Ford.

Once again the Dodges expanded their production facilities, purchasing 30 acres in Hamtramck, Michigan, in 1909. Their new building was capable of handling 5,000 production workers and was superbly designed for their type of production. The new complex also included a medical clinic with doctors and nurses in continuous attendance to treat injuries and health concerns on site. The Dodges even provided an internal welfare department with a $5 million dollar trust fund, and a well-equipped shop in which employees could work on personal or work-related projects on their own time. The Dodges displayed remarkable creativity and genuine concern for the welfare of their employees.

The Dodges had helped Ford attain enormous wealth in a relatively brief span of time, yet Henry Ford's enormous ego and passion for total control meant that a split between Ford and the Dodge brothers was inevitable.

In 1912 the Dodge brothers offered Ford the opportunity to purchase their company, which was ideally suited to Ford's production needs. Ford expressed interest but strung the Dodges along for several months without ever having any serious intention of purchasing their highly successful enterprise. At the same time, Ford himself was entertaining an $8 million offer to sell his company to William Durant, who owned Buick and Olds Motor Works. While negotiating with Durant, on one hand, Ford was quietly planning a new tractor division and the expansion of his present facilities.

The Dodges soon realized Ford's deception and that it was time to break with him. According to the specifications of their agreement, written notice was given to Ford on July 17, 1913, when John Dodge sent a letter to the Ford Motor Company formally ending their relationship. Then came the announcement that many insiders had predicted: "The Dodge Brothers, America's premier builder of automobile engines and components, confirmed plans that they would build a new automobile bearing the Dodge Brothers' marque." As the news traveled across the country, more than 20,000 letters and telegrams were received at Dodge headquarters requesting consideration for Dodge dealerships.

Dodge Becomes an Automaker

The new Dodge Brothers Motor Car Company was incorporated with stock valued at $5 million shared equally by John, named president, and by Horace, named vice president. Their existing factory, still committed to producing Ford

components, required refitting for auto manufacturing and extensive expansion to three times its present size, enclosing an area of nearly one and a half million square feet. The workers required to staff the new factory expanded to 7,500 by the start of auto production.

Horace Dodge was primarily responsible for the design of the Dodges' new four-cylinder, 35-horsepower engine. His motor turned out to be a superbly engineered product and remained Dodge's only production engine for the next 14 years. The *Michigan Manufacturer Journal* published a glowing forecast of the Dodges' new automobile stating, "When the Dodge Brothers new car comes out, there is no question that it will be the best thing on the market for the money. The Dodge Brothers are two of the best mechanics in Michigan and there is not an operation in their shop that they can't do with their own hands."

In spite of the enormous complexity of the task, the first Dodge automobile, a five-passenger touring model, rolled off the assembly line on November 14, 1914. In less than 16 months from the time they served notice canceling their contract with Ford, the Dodges were producing their own automobiles. What was equally amazing was that during the same period of time they continued to fulfill all their commitments to Ford, tripled the size of their factory, retooled every production machine, doubled their staff, and designed, engineered, tested, and produced a new high-quality automobile. It was a remarkable accomplishment in a highly complex industry and was universally praised by their astonished competition. However, there were also 120 other makes of automobiles in 1914, and the real test of their new automobiles was about to begin.

In 1914 Dodge Brothers' automobiles sold for $785, which was considerably more than the Model T as Ford continued to lower its retail price to bring it within reach of more buyers. John and Horace decided to concede the lower end of the market to Ford in favor of customers who preferred heavier, more durable vehicles. It was a prudent decision; Dodge reliability and quality attracted a significant following. The company was able to produce 250 vehicles in the few remaining months before the end of the calendar year in 1914. Their first full year of production was 1915 in which sales exceeded $35 million with an incredible volume of 45,000 vehicles, though Model T sales were at a quarter million. In 1916 volume increased to 70,000 vehicles and topped 101,000 in 1917. By 1919 Dodge had become America's third largest auto manufacturer behind Ford, which was selling more than 900,000 Model Ts, and the combined marques under the General Motors umbrella.

The immediate success of Dodge automobiles was based initially on the brothers' reputation for quality that they had established as a major component supplier. Their continued rise to prominence, however, was the result of their customers experiencing firsthand the quality built into the Dodge brothers' automobiles. Their cars were attractive, durable, reliable, and most important, they lived up to their customers' expectations.

Dodge Brothers Break with Ford

Purchasing an automobile was, for most buyers, a new and often risky experience. The Dodge brothers' slogan that their car "Speaks for Itself" caught on with the public because there was already trust in the Dodge name.

In 1916 the Dodges were still stockholders in the Ford Motor Company and counted on their annual dividends to reinvest in their business. Instead of the usual shareholder distribution, Ford announced plans to use the money to expand with a new plant along the Rouge River in Dearborn, Michigan.

Ford had started viewing his stockholders, whose initial investments had been repaid many times over, as "parasites." John and Horace saw through Ford's deception and brought a lawsuit to force Ford to distribute to the profits. A lengthy legal battle followed that wasn't settled until February 7, 1919, when the Michigan Supreme Court ruled in favor of the Dodges. The court determined that the Dodges' dividend share from Ford should amount to $2 million.

But Henry Ford was far from finished with his plans to drive out his stockholders. Perhaps with an inkling that the Dodge lawsuit was going against him, he suddenly resigned as president of Ford Motor Company on December 30, 1918, officially handing the reigns to his son, Edsel. Ford told reporters that he was planning to leave the Ford Motor Company and said that he had plans to use his tractor company, which he and Edsel owned, to produce a new automobile to compete with the

Model T. As the news leaked in March 1919, his scheme worked just as he had planned.

Because the buying public seemed ready to flock to Ford's new venture, the Dodge brothers and Ford's other stockholders agreed to be bought out at about a fourth of what their stock was probably worth. Agents working for Ford negotiated with John and Horace to purchase all of their shares of Ford Motor Company stock for $25 million. The Dodges were happy to receive the cash and remove themselves from Ford's deceptive activities. However, it was Henry Ford who ultimately achieved what he wanted all along. Through his maneuvering he was able to buy the remaining shares of stock for an additional $80 million and take total control of his company to operate as he wished.

Brothers in Arms

The Dodge brothers' enormous success was built on hard work, close attention to detail, and the desire to attract talented and dedicated employees. In addition to these attributes, the Dodges avoided borrowing money, which in retrospect may have been a bit too conservative for the operation of a multimillion-dollar manufacturer. Their products became synonymous with quality and were a constant representation of their honest approach to business. While these astute businessmen were able to stay on top of every detail of their operation, they were not perfect.

After every long day at work, it remained common practice for the brothers to stop at a neighborhood bar for a few drinks. As had always been the brothers' policy, when fights broke they held their ground but always seemed ready to pay for the damage that resulted. Another fault was that their total preoccupation with business left little time for regular involvement with their children or their wives. Granted, both John's second wife, Matilda (Ivy died in 1901), and Horace's wife, Anna, were given generous financial allowances to maintain their large homes without any restrictions and the children had the best of everything, attended the finest schools, and traveled frequently. Yet, while the brothers' unusual dedication to their professional priorities may have been the most critical factor in their remarkable business success, it also left a void that would deeply influenced the quality of their children's lives.

The trim and fast luxury yacht *Anna* was the first in an impressive series of custom-built yachts that Horace Dodge Sr. commissioned for his personal enjoyment.

Chapter Two

The Dodge Star Shines Brightly

It's hard to imagine the incredible transformation of status that took place in the lives of the

Dodge brothers and their families in a relatively short period. For John and Horace, though,

enormous financial wealth was never their ultimate goal. Had it been, they could have easily

stopped working shortly after Ford established his new motor car company and lived off

their shares of Ford stock. The Dodges, however, remained vibrant, full of creative ideas and

love for the potential fulfillment that the auto industry presented. They proved so adept at

whatever they set out to accomplish that there seemed to be no limit to what they could achieve. And, with their great wealth, they began to express their interest in pursuits outside of their business.

With their ever-increasing wealth, John and Horace built their own hunting and fishing retreats and commissioned some of America's most impressive yachts. Of the two inseparable brothers, Horace seemed to have the greatest interest in fast powerboats and luxurious yachts. Horace's two children, Delphine and Horace Jr., embraced their father's passion for boating.

Devoted to their business and to each other, John and Horace Sr. enjoyed each other's company, often at the expense of their wives, who were excluded from the brothers' close relationship. Their wives Matilda and Anna compensated for this void by accessing those things that the Dodge wealth made possible.

When Anna Dodge decided that it was time to move their comfortable home on Forest Street, she encouraged Horace to find a river-front lot on which to build a substantial home. Horace located a wonderful parcel in Grosse Pointe where Lake St. Clair flows into the Detroit River. The property also was close to the very exclusive Grosse Pointe Country Club. Since he would be building his new home nearby, it was only natural for Horace to apply for membership in the club. However, the entrenched members of the club summarily rejected Dodge's application. Many Detroiters were well aware of the stories regarding the Dodge brothers and their boisterous drinking style. The club's quick rejection so angered Horace that he retaliated by purchasing land adjacent to the country club. Then he leaked news that he planned to build a mansion on the land that was so grand that people would think the country club "was his garage."

Entering the Leisure Class

Horace hired the highly regarded architect Albert Kahn to design their magnificent Grosse Pointe home, an enormous project that was completed in 1910 just before Christmas. The style the Dodges selected was a variation of early–English Renaissance architecture constructed of deep red sandstone and aptly named "Rose Terrace." At the time it was completed, many considered it to be Detroit's most elegant mansion.

As mistress of this elegant new home, Anna Dodge found herself thrust into a social realm for which she was not at all prepared. Just furnishing such a home would take months of study and expert guidance. The furnishings from their previous home would be totally out of scale with the massive proportions of Rose Terrace. The logical person to help might have been her sister-in-law, Matilda Dodge. Unfortunately, their relationship was never close, and they were, in fact, becoming increasingly competitive. Neither could Anna Dodge's family provide the help she needed to acquire the good judgment that her new status required. Their understanding of good taste and fine furnishings was limited to vicarious experience through Anna. She was socially isolated, and it would take great fortitude on her part to educate herself on the necessary graces to furnish and operate Rose Terrace with the dignity expected of her. Both Anna and Horace would have to learn how to live graciously in the house that was a product of their new wealth.

Biographers Caroline Latham and David Agresta described Anna's challenge in this way:

The basic artificiality of the setting was underscored by the painful fact that Anna had no one to entertain in those magnificent rooms of her new house. Her only guests were poor relatives or business or political associates of her husband and his brother—and they, generally, preferred to do without female companionship. Then in her forties, with matronly clothes and few social graces, Anna lacked the ability to go out and make new friends. It took her several years to discover that essential strategy of the social climber—the charitable cause. Slowly, she learned to use Horace's contributions as a means of advancing her own social ambitions. She served as chairman of Red Cross Christmas Seal campaign and she entertained fellow committee members at luncheons. She capitalized on Horace's interest in music to get him to support the Detroit Symphony Orchestra (at one time, the musicians were almost literally on the Dodge Brother's payroll). He also gave money for the quick construction of a new, acoustically superior Symphony Hall, at which the family occupied a conspicuous box.

Developing a Passion for Boating

The Dodge brothers' fondness for boats went back to Niles, where they grew up along the St. Joseph River. As soon as they could afford the luxury of owning a fine yacht, they had a series of superb examples. In 1896 they built their own 52-foot steam yacht, *Lotus,* that was capable of speeds near 18 miles per hour and the fastest boat of its type on the Detroit River. Horace followed in 1903 with the 98-foot *Hornet,* whose Dodge-designed and -built 1,000-horsepower triple-expansion engine provided the sensational speed of 28 miles per hour. *Hornet II* was completed in 1910 and with its two Dodge-built engines reached 32 miles per hour. Built in 1914, their 190-foot yacht *Nokomis* was requested by the U.S. Navy to serve patrol duty along the Atlantic coast during World War I.

The navy accepted the yacht at a special ceremony attended by scores of prominent guests. The Dodges had become quite skilled at using their charitable donations to obtain extensive press coverage. The navy was pleased to use the *Nokomis* as a submarine patrol craft with a complement of 60 men. They valued the yacht at $200,000 and renamed it *Kwasind.* At the end of the war, it was sold to William Todd of the Todd Shipyards. Some of America's best-known celebrities would cruise aboard the refurbished yacht, including explorer Richard Byrd and aviators Wiley Post and Charles Lindbergh.

To replace his navy-bound *Nokomis,* Horace Dodge commissioned a new 582-ton steam yacht, which he also christened *Nokomis.* The new yacht was 63 feet longer than its predecessor, with a beam of 28 feet. At the time, it was also the largest privately owned steam yacht on the Great Lakes. Designed with comfortable staterooms and beautifully appointed salon areas to entertain guests, as well as two hotel-size galleys for extended cruising and entertaining, *Nokomis II* carried more than 350 tons of coal for nearly unlimited travel. Horace and his family took possession of the new yacht in Delaware and cruised north along the Atlantic coast into the mouth of the St. Lawrence River, through Lakes Ontario and Erie, and on to Detroit before anchoring at their home, Rose Terrace, on Lake St. Clair. *Nokomis II* made an impressive statement that the Dodges were beginning to understand the style associated

with great wealth. When the U.S. Navy requested *Nokomis II* for service in the war effort, the Dodges again graciously agreed. Upon its return, *Nokomis II* was renamed *Delphine* by the Dodges in honor of their daughter.

It didn't take long for Horace to dream up his next yacht: the magnificent 257-foot *Delphine II,* which took the mantle of being the largest on the Great Lakes. Dodge was deeply involved in every phase of the planning of *Delphine* and selected Henry J. Gielow, the noted New York naval architect, as its designer. The $2.25 million yacht still survives today and, as of the writing of this book in 2002, was just refurbished by its European owner. It displaces 1,700 tons, has five decks, and was intended for world travel in total luxury. Its eight guest staterooms average 14 feet by 14 feet in size, and each has a private or connecting bath. The owner's stateroom measures 20 feet by 25 feet with a lobby, a private entrance, and a private bath. The music room included a $60,000 organ. The salon deck features a smoking room, card room, lounge, and promenade, plus two 20-foot launches for the captain and crew, a 30-foot launch, and a 35-foot express runabout capable of 40 miles per hour for the owners. The yacht

Launched in 1917, the Dodge family's magnificent 247-foot yacht *Nakomis II* was turned over to the U.S. Navy for coastal patrol work during the final years of World War I.

has private quarters for a doctor, wireless operator, maids, and 10 personal servants. The crew numbered as many as 55 officers and men.

With a beam of 35 feet and a draft of 16 feet, 8 inches, the yacht is powered by twin four-cylinder, quadruple-expansion, oil-burning steam engines of 1,500 horsepower. It is equipped with three watertube boilers, similar to those used by the U.S. Navy. Fully loaded it carries 325,000 gallons of fuel oil and 200,000 gallons of fresh water.

The builder selected for the vessel was the Great Lakes Engineering Works in River Rouge, Michigan. Horace, who scheduled the keel to be set in place on June 17, 1920, anticipated that its top speed would be around 31 knots. (*Delphine II* was christened on April 2, 1921, by Delphine Dodge Cromwell; when the Dodges sold the former *Nokomis II*, renamed *Delphine*, they dropped the *II* from their new yacht and it became known simply as *Delphine*.)

Anna realized pleasure yachting was not enough and that her children needed to attend quality schools so they could make social contacts, which she suffered without, and receive superior educations. Delphine attended the school at the Convent of the Sacred Heart, considered the best in Grosse Pointe, before

it was decided that a boarding school would be more suitable. The Dodges' choice was the Springside School in Chestnut Hill, Pennsylvania.

Horace Jr. Puts on the Charm

Horace Jr. enrolled in the prestigious Manlius Military Academy near Syracuse in upstate New York. The new school, some 600 miles from Detroit, was selected when he was just 10 years old. His cousin, John Duval Dodge, was enrolled at the same time, with his mother, Matilda, having the similar goals of providing her son with a quality education, appreciation of the value of discipline, and association with other young men of prominent families. But John Duval's tenure at the Manlius School was cut short for a variety of disciplinary reasons. The school administration decided that he could not conform to their rules and should return home to Detroit. When the school refused to reinstate him, his parents enrolled him in the Culver Military Academy. His stay there also was rather brief, as John showed rebellious signs that would continue into adulthood.

Unlike his cousin, Horace Jr. was a bright youngster with a charming personal style that helped him make friends easily. While a student at Manlius, Horace took an unauthorized trip to

New York City arranged by his cousin, John Duval. Upon his return, Horace was dismissed for taking leave without permission. His parents pleaded to have their son reinstated and offered to give the school a sizeable donation to their building fund as a way to encourage the superintendent to reconsider his decision. A contribution was made and, within a short time, the superb Dodge Gymnasium was erected on the school's campus.

Young Horace was particularly skilled at convincing his mother to support virtually everything he wanted. He had a captivating personality and a delightful smile, and he conveyed an image of self-confidence. He frequently toyed with creative and interesting ideas, but rarely demonstrated the perseverance necessary to achieve meaningful success.

Horace Jr. completed his high school education at the Manlius, graduating in the class of 1920. He achieved the rank of Cadet Captain and was awarded the school's most prestigious award, The Order of the Phoenix, for his leadership in organizing boxing as a team sport in which he earned a varsity letter as a middle weight. His interest in boxing could very well have had its origins with the stories of the barroom fights in which his father and his uncle were famously involved; his success in organizing boxing as a team sport might have been an attempt to win favorable attention from his father. He also participated on the school's baseball and football squads and was known by the nickname "Barney."

Enrolled at Manlius when he was just 10 years old, Horace Jr. was nearly 20 when he graduated. Perhaps his extended residency indicates just how preoccupied his parents were with their own development and acceptance into Detroit society. By the time Horace Jr. returned to Detroit, his uncle had already died, while his father was battling the deadly influenza epidemic that had begun sweeping across the globe in 1918.

Living in High Society

The Dodges quickly learned that in Detroit, generosity to worthy causes could make a significant impression on the well-established, old-money families. Already skilled engineers, astute businessmen, and extremely wealthy, the Dodge brothers became exceptionally generous contributors to Detroit's cultural and civic institutions.

They always treated their employees very well, and their work on U.S. government contracts was exemplary and brought additional pride to Detroit's industries.

John and Horace Sr. were still too rough around the edges to be fully accepted by a few of Detroit's most exclusive groups and organizations, but their achievements were too remarkable to be overlooked much longer.

Detroit's Mayor George P. Codd (1905–1906) recognized John Dodge's leadership and management skills and appointed him to the Detroit Water Board. Dodge solved the city's problem of inadequate water pressure by building a new pumping station. It was not surprising that when he finally completed his term on the board in 1910, the water rates in Detroit were among the lowest in the country and the Detroit Water Plant was considered one of the most efficient in North America.

The Dodges also were active in the mayoral campaign of 1912 when their friend Oscar Marx ran for office. Marx won, and John Dodge, with his exemplary background in transportation, was appointed to the newly created Board of Street Railway Commissioners.

Anna and Matilda Dodge continued to become increasingly active in a growing number of cultural and civic programs, including the Salvation Army Refuge for Girls, the Women's Auxiliary, and the Detroit Federation of Women's Clubs. They became devoted to the new responsibilities that their husbands' wealth required of them and seemed to enjoy the challenge it presented.

Prominent Endorsements

Dodge Brothers Motor Car Company won several government contracts, including one in 1916 that was a special request from Brigadier General John Pershing for the War Department to purchase 250 Dodge vehicles for his command. Pershing made it clear that only his Dodge vehicles had successfully negotiated the rugged terrain in Mexico in raids against Pancho Villa. Pershing's endorsement provided a superb boost to the quality and performance of Dodge Brothers products.

Presidential candidate Charles Evan Hughes made a visit to the Dodge Brothers plant in 1916, as did many other prominent Americans. The

Dodge factory was symbolic of quality, success, and a bright future. It was also a model of excellent relationships between production workers and management.

Death at the Brothers' Door

On Friday, January 2, 1920, John and Horace arrived at Detroit's Michigan Central Railroad Station to begin their overnight trip to the National Automobile Show in New York City. The train arrived at New York's Grand Central Station the following morning, and the brothers went directly to the Ritz-Carlton Hotel to check in. From the hotel they walked with energetic strides to Grand Central Palace for the grand opening of the automobile exposition. They went directly to their Dodge Brothers exhibit area to see their display of the first enclosed Dodge four-door sedan. The smart, shiny black sedan looked wonderful under the Palace's special accent lighting. They enjoyed overhearing viewers praise the attractive appearance of the new Dodge vehicle. The factory was currently producing 500 cars a day to meet the growing demand for their cars. Business was, clearly, very good.

Together, John and Horace attended several special seminars at the auto show dealing with topics important to manufacturers, including the growing problem of auto theft. In 1919 more than 10,000 automobiles were stolen; it had become a major crime problem that automakers needed to address. Horace arrived at the seminar prepared to demonstrate his new detachable steering wheel. With this device auto owners could easily remove their steering wheel and take it with them or lock it in the car to deter a thief. Although it was never adapted, it was another example of the how the Dodges were always closely involved in the needs of the industry.

The next morning neither Horace nor John felt well. Their conditions were such that John summoned a doctor who told both men they had a case of the "grippe." Horace was the sicker of the two and decided that he needed to stay in bed, which was so unusual that John became deeply concerned. He quickly requested that a specialist be summoned and remained with his brother. As additional New York doctors were called and John's worries grew, he sent for their personal physician from Detroit, along with both

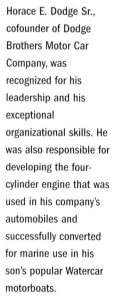

Horace E. Dodge Sr., cofounder of Dodge Brothers Motor Car Company, was recognized for his leadership and his exceptional organizational skills. He was also responsible for developing the four-cylinder engine that was used in his company's automobiles and successfully converted for marine use in his son's popular Watercar motorboats.

of their wives. By this time John, too, was becoming quite ill. His condition declined very rapidly. Several doctors were at the brothers' bedsides as nurses bathed the patients with tepid water to reduce their fevers.

Horace remained seriously ill but passed the crisis and began slowly improving. John, however, rapidly grew worse and fell in and out of unconsciousness. His damaged lungs filled with fluid and his breathing was labored. The medical team didn't move either brother from their hotel suite because their conditions were so guarded. They couldn't stop John's condition from worsening, and by the end of the day on January 14, the strong, robust man of 55 was dead.

Matilda's grief was complicated when she also developed the early signs of influenza. Horace was still very ill and remained in New York with Anna at his side while Matilda accompanied her husband's body back to Detroit in their special railroad car. Upon her return, Matilda became so ill fighting her own influenza that she was unable to attend her husband's funeral. Thousands of saddened Detroiters paid their respects to one of their most successful citizens and one of America's most successful automotive pioneers.

Influenza reached epidemic proportions in several major American cities. Municipal offices, theater performances, and schools closed as public services were discontinued due to shortages of nurses and police officers. By mid-February the worst period of the epidemic passed and Horace slowly regained enough strength to return to Detroit. He was thinner and very weak and would suffer occasional relapses. The loss of his brother left him depressed and despondent. His daughter, Delphine, who was engaged to be married to James Cromwell, continued with her plans and was married in June, followed by an extensive trip abroad. In the fall, Horace Jr., home from Manlius Military Academy for less than a year, announced his plans for marriage when he and Lois Knowlson became engaged.

Anna and Horace Sr. decided that it was time for them to spend some time together at their winter home in Palm Beach. Just before their departure, the elder Horace called his attorney to run through several items that needed to

be addressed and to draw up a revised will. The following day Anna, Horace, and his personal physician boarded their private rail car and headed south. A week after their arrival in Florida, Horace began to hemorrhage unexpectedly. He received immediate medical support, but the 52-year-old Horace Sr. died on December 10, 1920, of atrophic hepatic cirrhosis. Incredibly, the vigorous and talented Dodge brothers were both gone within a year of each other. The auto industry and America lost two remarkable leaders when they were still at the peak of their creative accomplishments.

Dodge Family Sells Dodge Brothers

A few days before leaving for Palm Beach, Horace Dodge Sr. had named his trusted assistant and longtime friend, Frederick J. Haynes, the new president of Dodge Brothers. A Cornell University graduate and a key figure in the Franklin Car Company of Syracuse, New York, before joining Dodge Brothers in 1912, Haynes was a superb choice to oversee the company.

Under Haynes' leadership, by 1924 the corporation had grown by nearly 36 percent with sales of $217 million and a volume of 225,000 vehicles. When it finally became clear to Anna that Horace Jr. held no aspirations to a management position with his father's automobile firm, there was no longer any necessity for her or her sister-in-law Matilda to continue holding ownership of the huge, complex operation. The New York investment firm of Dillon Read offered a bid of $146 million to purchase Dodge Brothers. When accepted, the deal became the largest single private-business cash transaction in the United States up to that time.

When Dodge stock was offered for sale to the public, the new owners realized a profit of $28 million, and the *New York Post* reported, "Never before in the financial history of the country has so widespread response been given to a public offering." Anna Dodge still believed in the company's vast potential and purchased 60,000 shares of stock at the initial offering. In the spring of 1928, automaker Walter P. Chrysler purchased the Dodge Brothers Corporation for $230 million and called it "one of the soundest acts of my life."

Two well-regarded vintage race boats, Caleb Bragg's *Baby Bootlegger* and Horace Dodge Jr.'s *Baby Horace III*, run side by side with both boats looking as good as they did when they were built. *Thomas Mittler*

Chapter Three

Horace Elgin Dodge Jr.

Shortly after returning to the Manlius Military Academy after the New Year's school break in 1920, Horace Jr. was told of his Uncle John's death and his father's serious illness. He joined his family in Detroit for his uncle's funeral and to spend time with his father during a portion of his convalescence. He returned to the academy after a few weeks at home to attend classes and finish his assignments prior to graduation in June.

In many ways his prep school dormitories were far more familiar surroundings to him than his own bedroom in Rose Terrace, yet Horace Jr. was nonetheless eager to return to Detroit after so many years away from home. Most of all he missed the rivers and lakes near Detroit, where he could take pleasure in his boats and racing.

In addition to automobiles, Detroit was a national center for boat building. Chris Smith, Gar Wood, John Hacker, and Ed Gregory were all Detroit-based boat builders who were already famous for their record-setting performances as race-boat pilots. Horace couldn't wait for the opportunity to compete with these established champions.

During the summer of 1920, Gar Wood shipped two of his celebrated race boats, *Miss Detroit V* and *Miss America*, to England to compete in the British International Trophy (known as the Harmsworth Trophy). When news of Wood's runaway victory was received, he was viewed as a national hero and brought great recognition to Detroit. Gar Wood became famous throughout the world of racing as the speedboat king and a hero to young Horace Dodge, the person whom he would like to emulate. Now that he was finished with school and living in Detroit, Horace Jr.'s desire to exceed Gar Wood's speed records evolved first into an enthusiastic passion and then into a lifelong obsession.

A Son Out of Control

It was always assumed that Horace Jr. would enter the automobile business even though he possessed neither the mechanical aptitude nor the resourceful determination that were vital aspects of his father's and his uncle's remarkable success. The unexpected death of his father lessened his interest in the car business even further, but Horace Jr. felt an obligation to his father and to his family to make a reasonable effort to see if the automotive industry suited him.

Within a month of his father's death, 20-year-old Horace was arrested twice for speeding and driving so recklessly as to endanger passengers at a bus stop. Displaying a deputy's badge that had been given to his father, Horace first threatened to arrest the police officer for interfering with county business and then reached for his pocket, where he had a gun to back up the badge. A tussle ensued and a bullet was accidentally fired into the ground. Horace was whisked into custody but later released due to the "unfortunate misunderstanding."

Horace agreed to spend some time in Florida with his mother as they coped with the loss of the driving force in their lives. Both Dodge brothers—who had made all the major decisions for their two families—as well as their huge industry, were gone. Their families were left with millions of dollars, huge homes, enormous yachts, and little knowledge of the industry that made all their wealth possible. Young Horace hardly knew his father, let alone how to run the complex company that his father and uncle had created.

Soon after arriving at the family's Palm Beach winter home with his mother, Horace's grief abated and he indulged in all the excitement available to him there. He spent time with a group of socially prominent young drinkers who took unusual pleasure in attending all-night parties. His attraction to these new friends and their irresponsible activities worried his mother. Horace enjoyed a very favorable relationship with his mother, but he really needed his father's strong influence to keep him focused. With Horace Sr. gone, Horace Jr.'s drinking and irresponsible behavior grew nearly out of control.

When Horace's fiancée, Lois Knowlson, and her parents made a brief visit to Palm Springs, Anna was delighted. Anna was very fond of Lois and felt that her presence in Palm Beach might have a positive influence on her son's behavior. She successfully encouraged Lois to stay on awhile longer, hoping to keep Horace away from the hard-drinking parties. Having Lois there brought a positive change in Horace's behavior, but his predisposition to frivolous activities, heavy drinking, and late-night parties persisted. Anna greatly hoped that his eventual marriage to Lois would bring stability.

A Spectacular Launch

It was early April before Horace and his mother returned to Detroit. One of their first activities was the christening of his father's completed 257-foot yacht, *Delphine II*, at the Great Lakes Engineering Works at River Rouge. This was the yacht that his father planned and commissioned after allowing the U.S. Navy to take possession of *Nakomis II* during the final years of World War I. Hundreds of family friends and curious onlookers gathered for the occasion. The yacht was constructed on skids that were designed for a spectacular sideways launch into the river rather than the more traditional stern-first launching. Photographers were stationed in several locations to capture on film the sight of the huge and elegant *Delphine II* sliding sideways across greased timbers.

Yachting magazine covered the launching and reported, "The lines of *Delphine* are particularly sweet, with an easy sweep from stem to stern, broken only by the raised foc's'le head, which is on the same level as the saloon or promenade deck. Her sheer is very moderate but graceful. She is the largest yacht in gross tonnage ever built in this country and is one of the largest steam yachts ever built anywhere. Curiously enough, her nativity is an inland city and her launching occurred on the shores of the Great Lakes."

The launching was spectacular. *Delphine II* was the largest privately owned yacht on the Great Lakes, limited in its length only by the capacity of the size of the Welland Canal locks. It was another impressive triumph for the now-deceased Dodge brothers.

The next family event for the Dodges was Horace's wedding to Lois Knowlson, planned for June 1, 1921. As a measure of respect for the recent death of Horace's father, the family agreed that a small, quiet wedding at the home of Lois' parents would be appropriate and in good taste. Although Horace was just 21 years old, Anna was pleased about his decision to marry Lois and hoped that she would provide a stable home and encourage him to take greater interest in assuming a position in the Dodge Brothers Motor Car Company.

Following their quiet wedding, the young couple traveled to Europe for an extended honeymoon. Upon their return to Detroit, Horace reported directly to the Pattern Shop at the Dodge factory "to learn the work from the ground up," as he told reporters during a brief interview. In spite of his apparent good intentions to learn all that was necessary to become a significant part of the automobile business, it quickly became a struggle for Horace to stay motivated. The prospects of looking ahead to a successful career in the auto industry did not improve over time. Horace's interest and desire to remain with Dodge Brothers declined steadily, as his lack of skill became more self-evident.

Horace Jr.'s Growing Obsession

In the spring of 1922, shortly before their first wedding anniversary, Horace and Lois became parents of a baby daughter. The young parents named their daughter Delphine for Horace's sister, of whom they were both very fond. Horace spent much of the summer participating in a number of local races in his 20-foot racing hydroplane, *Baby Holo*. In early September, while the boat-racing season was still very active, Horace entered the Mayor Couzens' Detroit Trophy Race with *Baby Holo*. In spite of the constant rain, nearly 10,000 spectators crowded the shore as Horace roared ahead of his only opponent in the first lap. He held his lead until the fourth lap, when *Baby Holo* dove into a large swell, causing the engine to stall out and nearly sinking the boat before he was towed back to shore.

Later that month Horace shipped *Baby Holo* to Buffalo, New York, to compete for an International Trophy Regatta on the Niagara River. In this important race Horace's boat designer, Bill "Oregon Kid" Crowley, not only drove *Baby Holo* to victory but established two world records for the 2,200-ci single-engine hydroplane class. Crowley was well prepared to handle the unusual boat and had it in top running condition, driving an excellent series with an average speed of 64.1 miles per hour for a 5-mile lap, the first of the two world records. He set the second record for averaging 62.5 miles per hour for a 30-mile heat. Crowley's significant record-setting races elevated *Baby Holo*'s status to that of a highly respected race boat.

Horace celebrated the victory for several days, causing his mother to worry that racing and partying were more important to Horace than his work-related responsibilities. Horace's behavior also convinced her that the nearly $50 million under her control was best left out of her son's hands for the time being as she tried to influence him to straighten up.

After the significant victories in Buffalo, Horace wanted, more than ever, to indulge himself in the same excitement and fame that Gar Wood was experiencing. Wood was getting old by competitive racer standards—he was 42, twice Horace's age—and soon would be past his prime. Horace became convinced that the opportunities to go head to head with Wood were getting shorter. He needed to beat Wood himself or racing journalists of the period like Harry Leduc and Everett Morris would always claim that Wood was the best boat racer of all time. Horace was confident that he could exceed Wood's splendid accomplishments and that *he* could become the greatest international race-boat champion of all time.

Young Horace became obsessed with the opportunity to challenge his hero in a race. The huge endowment established by his father provided more than enough capital to meet the large financial requirements to fulfill any racing goal Horace desired. He was a young man of exceptional self-confidence and possessed a warm and captivating personality. He was, however, still an inexperienced young man whose desires were far greater than his dedication to the essential preparations that were required to achieve them.

When pushed by his wife and his mother to express his preferences for a suitable career, Horace always pointed to profound interest in boats and the thrills of racing. The successful accomplishments of Gar Wood always seemed to be a part of these discussions. He envied Wood's triumphant victories and the joy he imagined Wood received by creating exciting new boats year after year. To Horace, Wood's life not only seemed perfect, it was a model that he wanted to emulate by enjoying great wealth, remaining socially prominent, becoming commodore of the Detroit Yacht Club, flying his own airplane, and owning his own successful and profitable boat-building firm.

Capitalizing on the Boating Fever

With thanks to Gar Wood, Chris Smith, and John Hacker, Detroit was becoming the national hub for boat building just as it was for the auto industry. The euphoria for boats and racing was growing as rapidly in the Midwest as it was in the East. Horace could visualize his own bright future following a path similar to Gar Wood and then surpassing him completely as Dodge became the new speedboat king. All he needed was to establish his own special niche that would attract people to his boats. He was confident that his chances of surpassing Wood as Detroit's most successful racer were virtually assured.

Using the vast estate left by his father, he could employ the finest designers, use the most powerful engines, and even build the boats in his own factory. Horace was certain that Wood's racing career was approaching its twilight period. The success Horace desired was, in his mind, simply a matter of time and money—and he had both on his side.

Anna Dodge still preferred a secure career for her son in the family's auto business. However, she felt that it was important for him to remain motivated by something in which he was interested and at which he could excel. Horace always made a convincing case for what he wanted, and she was no match for his charm and persistence. In building his case for entering the boat business, he pointed out that the very same techniques that proved successful in manufacturing automobiles were absent in nearly every small boat-building operation. He noted that boats were built one at a time by a crew of men, rather than manufactured in production lines by specialists skilled in specific functions. This outmoded and inefficient style resulted in high prices, he argued, and very small profit margins. He pleaded to his mother that his ideas could change boat construction forever. Anna Dodge was impressed with her son's logic and his apparent research. She was ready to let him test his theory. It was agreed that he could begin preparations for organizing his company immediately with her pledge of full financial support.

Under Mother's Watchful Eye

In 1923, the members of the Grosse Point Country Club decided to sell their lakefront property and their clubhouse that adjoined Rose Terrace. Anna bid $625,000 for the property, planning to build a new home for Horace and his family in another obvious attempt to exert some measure of control over her son's behavior and restrain his excessive drinking. She was also uneasy over the lack of restraint both Horace and his sister, Delphine, demonstrated when granted access to large sums of money. She decided that she would do whatever was necessary to protect the Dodge estate until stronger signs of fiscal responsibility by her two children surfaced.

Horace's lavish new 28-room home was built right next to Rose Terrace and named Gray House. Despite the responsibility of the new house, Horace remained deeply involved in motorboat racing, and it seemed that his only other interest was attending lavish parties with unusual frequency. His fun-loving, jovial manner made him a welcome guest with Detroit's social set.

Horace remained determined to become a major motorboat producer and to top Gar Wood as the next race-boat king. To make his plan work, he envisioned employing efficient, straight-line production techniques—similar to those used on automobile assembly lines—to build quality that could be sold at very affordable prices. He was convinced he could put working-class families in boats the same way his father and his uncle put them in cars. His first challenge was convincing his wife, Lois, and his mother, Anna, that his plan was reasonable and worthy. It was critical for him to gain the financial backing that only his mother could supply.

Horace was at his diplomatic best when he sought his mother's support. Anna thought that his production-line approach to boat building made sense and that he had a reasonable chance for success. Horace also pointed out how much his father loved boats and that victory in racing was an important way of promoting his plan. Finally, he cited Gar Wood's status as a respected boat builder, as a racing champion, and as a civic leader in Detroit as the model for success he wished to follow.

A Night in Venice

With his mother's support assured, Horace Jr. had enough time to secure a booth at the 1923 National Motor Boat Show in New York City to announce that the Horace E. Dodge Boat Works in Detroit was about to revolutionize boating in America. He prepared an attractive flyer announcing his plans, hoping to stir enough interest to get his business off to a successful start. The only asset he had to bring to the event was the Dodge name, but it was enough to provide him with enormous, instant recognition.

The boat business would, technically, be his mother's business. Horace even refused to take a salary from the boat business for fear that it might disqualify his amateur status in race-boat competition. With his course set to carve out an exciting niche in powerboats, Horace was still careful not to stray too far from the automobile business. His new line of boats was named Watercars and was initially marketed through Dodge Brothers automobile dealers nationwide.

To celebrate his new boat-building career, Horace and Lois hosted a lavish costume house party themed "A Night in Venice." Horace used the grounds of Rose Terrace overlooking Lake St. Clair to create his own version of Venice's wonderful St. Mark's Square with street café tables for all his guests. On the waterfront, their magnificent yacht, *Delphine II,* floated gracefully at anchor with lighted lanterns strung from its masts and fireworks launched from its deck. It was the party of the decade, with Horace dressed as Mephistopheles in red satin knee breeches, a scarlet hood, and horns. The party was such a remarkable event that it became a Horace Dodge tradition for several years, still remembered as one of Detroit's great social events.

Horace spent $50,000 that night to entertain his guests. Included on the guest list were Murlen and Garfield Wood, who, along with each couple in costume, had their photograph taken with their host. The photo made a remarkable image with Horace dressed as Mephistopheles, confidently contemplating his plan to dethrone the speedboat king with whom he was being photographed.

Creating the Watercar

Horace prepared his promotional flyer for the New York boat show by describing to his satisfaction the concepts of standardization and production lines. Realizing that his new approach to manufacturing high-quality, standardized boats that were affordable to the average working family might sound unrealistic, he settled on an approach that made so much sense to him that he couldn't wait to share it with the crowds in New York City. The brochure read:

Since the beginning, the motorboat industry has suffered a serious handicap, namely, the fact that the vast majority of the boats have to be built to order. There is every likelihood that if the automobile industry had followed this method the number of cars in use today would have been many millions less than it is. The success of Ford, Dodge, Cadillac, Pierce-Arrow, Packard and others has been largely due to the fact that their makers have established one or two definite

chassis models. They are slow to make radical changes in their designs. This obvious recipe for successful manufacturing has been unknown in the motor boat field. And herein lies the revolutionary feature of the Dodge Boat Works. The new Dodge Watercar will be a standardized model that covers a wide range of boating uses. By concentrating on this model, we can produce it with every luxury and advantage at a low price hitherto thought impossible for a boat of this type.

I feel that in building Dodge Watercars and using thoroughly standardized automobile manufacturing methods, except for the special limitations motor boat construction entails, we are fully prepared for the wholesale public adoption of the water for recreational purposes. And if that happens, and I'm sure it will, it will be because the motor boat builders have learned by the experience of the automobile industry how to build high class boats by standardized production methods offering economy unobtainable any other way. In other words boats of the future will be like the Dodge Watercars of today.

Horace admired the runabout design that Martin Draeger of the Racine Boat Company had developed and was building. Dodge decided to meet with Draeger and was pleased to hear his like-minded and firm position on the need for standardized boats and the importance of production lines to reduce construction costs. Draeger provided drawings, and the two decided that the 22-foot runabout hull was ideal for the type of boat Dodge wanted to build. Details were reviewed and refined so that Dodge had a design with which he was comfortable.

The boat would be called the Watercar to take full advantage of Dodge's important automotive background; the unique name would draw a clear distinction between his boats and all others on the market. The initial Watercar also took several design cues from Dodge automobiles. The Watercar incorporated long-deck styling with the engine forward of the driver. The seating was automobile-style, with the front and rear seats located in a single cockpit behind the engine compartment and protected by a large, attractive windshield. The dash instruments and controls also were

modeled after the style found in automobiles. When the optional folding top was fastened in place, it gave the craft a profile much like that of a typical automobile. To complete the automobile connection, Dodge planned to use a marine conversion of the superb Dodge Brothers four-cylinder automotive engine that his father developed that would provide 35 horsepower and anticipated speeds around 20 miles per hour.

In addition, Horace negotiated with his associates at Dodge to sell his boats through Dodge Brothers dealerships across the country. Draeger provided an attractive drawing for the 1923 boat show in New York so that Dodge could actually have a design on paper to show potential prospects. However, at the boat show, Dodge's Watercar was still only a drawing and a dream.

Living Up to Expectations

At the show Dodge passed out flyers to anyone who indicated any interest in his new boat. He had little trouble gathering a receptive audience willing to listen to his application of automotive production methods to the building of a standardized boat. The more Dodge described his plans, the more convinced he became that he had hit upon a profound revelation. Upon returning to Detroit from the 1923 National Motor Boat Show, Horace found his mother delighted with his motivation and agreeable that his approach to boat construction had merit. Knowing it was necessary to keep him involved and productive, she wanted to do everything she

could to support his new endeavor. She also agreed that they needed to live up to the established reputation of the well-respected Dodge name by doing everything on a grand scale and avoiding failure.

Anna realized that the expectations would be higher for them and that success would require high-profile advertising, an efficient and well-equipped factory with extensive materials storage, railroad access, and a river location to facilitate water testing. Dodge knew that he had his mother's full support and she knew that it might be an expensive adventure with a good chance at being highly successful.

Using the feedback from the crowds at the New York boat show, the Draeger and Horace Dodge design was refined so that production could begin in the spring. Yet so much had to be done, and time was running short if he wanted to have an inventory of new boats in time for the 1924 National Motor Boat Show.

Dodge needed to spend enormous amounts of time selecting a suitable factory, equipping it with the proper machinery, hiring a skilled staff, and preparing ad layouts and news releases while finalizing the Watercar's construction details. He conceded that the only way he could ensure a timely supply of new boats was to use an outside contractor for initial production. Yet even that task wasn't easy.

Finding a well-established and well-equipped woodworking shop capable of building dozens of 22-foot mahogany runabouts was a serious

This early illustration of the 22-foot Watercar was prepared for the 1923 New York Boat Show to provide visitors with a more precise idea of its unique design features and to illustrate the forward location of the dependable Dodge four-cylinder engine.

challenge. Dodge looked into several established boat builders, including Defoe Shipbuilding in Bay City, Michigan, where a prototype pattern hull was prepared. However, he soon realized that traditional boat-building shops were unwilling to experiment with the production style he insisted upon. The only shops that could handle a job of such magnitude and precision were those that produced frames and components for automobile bodies. So Horace quietly decided to give the job to the Racine Manufacturing Company in Wisconsin, fabricators of wooden components for automobile bodies. It proved to be a prudent choice, as well as an example of the vast financial strength of the Dodge wealth.

The Racine Manufacturing Company was a firm apart from Draeger's Racine Boat Company. In accepting the Dodge contract to build 111 of the 22-foot Watercars, Racine Manufacturing agreed to hire Draeger to act as the on-site superintendent for the project. The Dodge contract also included the exact completion date for the work and a requirement for using production line procedures similar to those the Dodges anticipated using in their own factory, which was under construction on Atwater Street in Detroit.

The subcontracting provided an opportunity for Dodge and Draeger to evaluate production techniques prior to setting up their own lines. And there was one more requirement: Dodge insisted that the entire operation be conducted in the strictest confidence without any publicity related to the subcontract. Here was a fledgling boat company with enough financial power to contract quietly for 111 fully equipped boats to be produced and delivered before the first one was even sold or water-tested. It was a remarkable circumstance.

Proving Dodge's Theory
Martin Draeger's approach to modernizing boat construction conformed perfectly to Horace's belief that standardized boats could be produced more efficiently by adapting the modern techniques employed by automobile manufacturers. Draeger, in fact, expressed his absolute dedication to standardization as a key factor for reducing construction costs, stating:

As long as the typical boat builder will build any type of boat that he is asked to

build to suit the thousand and one whims and fancies of a buyer, he will continue to be on the way to the poorhouse. Boat builders are the poorest paid of any highly skilled craftsman. Year after year the typical boat builder is hoping to emerge out of the rut. The best that he has accomplished by the end of a season of hard labor is that he is able to pay off his previous year's debts and square himself with creditors to establish credit for another year of the same. And so it goes, year after year.

Shortly after Draeger's successful experience building the 111 22-foot Dodge Watercars using this new approach, he published a fascinating report of his experience in *Rudder* and *Boating* magazines to encourage other boat builders to rethink their methods of construction. In one of his articles entitled "Build or Manufacture?" he wasted little time making his point to his readers, explaining, "Manufacturing and standardization are the remedies. By manufacturing I mean building by machinery and the elimination of all possible handwork. Standardization would mean the adoption of one, two or three types of boats and a strict commitment to these designs. Once this determination has been made and the builder has perfected his construction methods to specialize on this particular type, he will be surprised to see how effective it will be to reduce the cost of construction."

Draeger made it clear that he did not blame the customer for the lack of standardization or the style of construction that boat builders continued to practice; he placed the full responsibility on the shoulders of boat builders themselves. He wrote further:

Let's look at the situation from a buyer's point of view, or better still, let's step into the buyer's position and contemplate buying a new boat. If I were asked to pay the existing prices for a modern, medium priced runabout, I would get a shock! I would certainly hesitate, then quickly give up the thought of ever enjoying this wonderful sport. I don't want to create the impression that boats are not worth the price—not at all. In fact many boats are too low in price for all the effort, pain and labor that has been

The interior of the East Lycaste Street factory is shown with the finishing room located to the right and two 22-foot Watercars in the final stages of completion. Note the shallow waterline depth at the transom due to the forward location of the engine.

put into them. So why do boat builders continue to hand craft boats instead of manufacturing them? All I can see ahead for those who persist in the old methods is a funeral with no mourners left behind so far as the buyers are concerned.

At this point in his article, Draeger related his experiences supervising the construction of the 22-foot Dodge Watercars. The job called for the boats to be completely finished and ready to launch and run in a specified time frame. The contractor, Racine Manufacturing, operated a modern woodworking facility with a highly skilled labor force. However, they were all automobile body workers, not experienced boat builders.

How Standardization Worked

Martin Draeger began the project by hiring the only two available boat builders with experience whom he could locate for this contract. Their immediate goal was to build the complete construction frame that would be used for patterns. This included every piece that comprised the boat's wooden components except for its planking and decking.

Draeger and the two boat carpenters constructed the prototype 22-foot Watercar, the "pattern boat," by hand. Every piece of this first hull had to be perfectly fit because it became the pattern for the parts of subsequent production boats. The shop foreman reminded them several times of this important fact. It took three weeks to tool up the shaper moulds and jigs for production of the standardized components. When the pattern boat was finished, it was carefully inspected, given final approval, and then disassembled for the pattern shop to begin production.

In June 1923, a crew of workers was assigned to produce the Dodge Watercars under Draeger's supervision. The single element that the new work crew had in common was their total lack of boat-building experience. The two experienced boat builders who assisted Draeger in building the pattern boat were promoted to the role of instructors. It became their responsibility to train the work crew to prepare set-ups properly and to handle all the framing. As the work progressed, additional workers were assigned until the total number of automobile body builders involved in manufacturing the boats grew to 52.

The first few weeks of work progressed slowly as each crew became familiar with the job requirements. As each man became more comfortable with his assignment, production picked up steadily, and soon the operation was moving along as anticipated. The final output produced two completed boats each day with motors installed and upholstered seats in place; all that was left was to add gas to the tank and touch the starter. Inside of two and a half months, they built 110 high-quality, standardized, mahogany runabouts to precise specifications with a crew of workers who had virtually no previous boat-building experience. It was a significant triumph for Horace Dodge as well as Martin Draeger. Their new approach to modernizing boat building passed its first test.

In his article "Build or Manufacture?" Draeger described the experience:

The boat construction began on June 1st and by August 15th all one hundred and eleven Watercars were completed, ready to run, with all the fixins, upholstery, motors, n'everything. We found that by letting each group of men do just a certain kind of work, they quickly became expert at it. The framers were followed by the side plankers. The riveters came next, to be followed by the bottom plankers and the bottom riveters. Young boys put in 3,156 wood plugs on the sides and bottom. Down the line the hulls went to the dressers. Then into the joiner department, ready for the deck beams, decking, coaming, cockpit sheathing, floor boards, etc. Everything was timed and we used only the right number of men put to a certain job so as to avoid delays.

It was a remarkable accomplishment that clearly demonstrated to every boat builder ready to listen that Horace Dodge's revolutionary new production approach was efficient, cost effective, and now proven as a way to maintain quality standards and increase volume. Dodge was off to an impressive start in the boat business. Equally important was his mother's pleasure in what had been accomplished with the successful application of what Horace had been able to glean from his scant automobile production background. She was much more confident about his decision to manufacture boats and was ready to provide additional funds for his new enterprise. Still, despite the triumph, none of the new 22-footers was built in the Dodge's brand-new Atwater Street factory in Detroit, nor had any been delivered to a customer.

An early production model of the 22-foot Watercar is water-tested in 1923. The hull was based on a Martin Draeger design and built by the Racine Manufacturing Company in Racine, Wisconsin, for the Dodge Boat Works.

From this angle, the attractive curves that make the 22-foot Watercar *Dazzle* so appealing to boating enthusiasts are very evident. *Lindsey Hopkins III*

Below: The early Dodge instrument panel for the 22-foot Watercar was similar to the one used in the Dodge brothers' automobiles of the same period. The Watercar was powered by the Dodge brothers' four-cylinder automobile engine. *Lindsey Hopkins III*

While the new boats were being built, Dodge concentrated on organizing, staffing, and equipping the Atwater Street factory. No other boat builder in America could order and build 100 new powerboats before the first one was ever sold to a customer. It was a stunning example to the entire industry of the clout that Dodge could apply to an idea with his wealth.

Carving Out His Niche

Gaining more confidence with each passing day, Dodge began to announce his plans in a series of articles and advertising layouts in many of the major boating magazine's. The 22-foot boat was always identified as "*the Watercar*" in promotional layouts, with the stated primary goal to "build a boat that would be within reach of the average family and yet be, in every sense of the word, a superior boat." In nearly every article and ad placed by Horace, great emphasis was put on the important relationship between the success of Dodge Brothers automobiles and the Watercars' exclusive use of the reliable Dodge engines. The trade name Watercar was important to Dodge because it was a continuing reminder to the public that his boat's concept

was based on the enormous success of the popularly priced Dodge cars.

Dodge employed several interesting advantages over established boat builders and cleverly used each one to distance his boats from the competition. He wanted to be viewed as a refreshing manufacturer to boaters and not part of the old establishment. He wanted to be associated with the excitement of the auto industry and perceived as ready to revolutionize boat building. Because of his connections with the

Dodge Brothers Automobile Dealers Association, Dodge car dealers were given the opportunity to become Watercar dealers if they chose to do so.

Since the new boats were powered primarily by the 35-horsepower Dodge four-cylinder automobile engines, this arrangement also meant that Dodge Brothers dealers could provide engine service and repairs if required, instantly creating a nationwide service center network for the new boats. The plan was unparalleled in the world of boating and gave Watercars immediate credibility to potential buyers. All at once, this spanking new firm was able to announce the largest network of marine dealers in the entire industry.

Dodge made the following statement to the press soon after the arrangements with the Dodge Brothers automobile dealers were set in place:

In the case of the Horace E. Dodge Boat Works, the organization is definitely and permanently established, and the service question—the greatest obstacle to quantity production and general use of pleasure boats—is settled for all time. It is a foregone conclusion that there will always be a Dodge Brothers Dealer in every city or town of the slightest consequence and it is equally obvious, in view of the importance which Dodge Brothers place on service, that these dealers will always be in a position to give prompt advice or assistance on any question affecting the operation of the Dodge Watercar. This advantage is of singular importance to the boat owner. It enables a novice to buy with perfect assurance of complete satisfaction, as he will always be within easy reach of an authorized service station regardless of where his course may take him.

Dodge's Watercar sales literature continued to emphasize the importance and security of their relationship with the Dodge Brothers corporation and to point out how much the Dodge Watercar and Dodge automobiles had in common, including controls, instruments, and the engine itself. Watercar brochures stressed that the public could obtain prompt delivery of a speedy and trustworthy boat from any Dodge Brothers dealer anywhere in the country. It was a powerful consideration for any potential boat buyer. It also provided Dodge with an enormous running start as he entered the marketplace.

A Spectacular Return

Dodge had taken full advantage of his family's financial strength to lend credibility to his new approach to boat manufacturing. When he attended the 1923 National Motor Boat Show it was, primarily, to sample the market and reveal some of his ideas. Now confident that his concepts were sound, he was determined to return to New York the following year with the new boat that reflected everything he projected.

Dodge reserved a prime location for the 1924 show and returned in spectacular fashion. His gleaming mahogany 22-foot Watercar sport runabout was the talk of the event and received excellent reviews from all of the marine writers in attendance. Priced at $2,250, the first Watercars were 22 feet, 2 inches in length and 21 feet, 8 inches at the waterline with a 5-and-a-half-foot beam, a 16-inch draft, and a total displacement of 2,500 pounds. Planking was of Honduras mahogany, although the initial brochure left open the possibility of using African, Philippine, or Mexican mahoganies as well. Dodge was also quick to point out that his first-year production plans called for a larger volume output than ever before attained by any boat builder.

Dodge distributed his 12-page brochure with its detailed specifications, 12 photographs of the Watercar, and a lengthy narrative describing its virtues along with the advantages of its Dodge automotive heritage and the wisdom of its developer. It was identified as *the* Watercar, giving the impression that this boat would be the sole model to carry this special trade name.

A large sign at the Dodge display trumpeted, "A new achievement in Boat Building." Below the sign was the following description:

> *Ten years ago Horace E. and John F. Dodge built the vital parts for more than a half million automobiles and determined to build a car of their own—a car that would be within the reach of the average family and yet be, in every sense of the word, a real automobile. Two years ago, Horace E. Dodge, son of one of the founders of Dodge Brothers, determined to build a boat that would be within the reach of the average family, and yet be, in every sense of the word, a superior boat.*

A universally respected naval architect and a professor at the prestigious Webb Institute, George Crouch surprised the boating world by accepting a position with Horace Dodge Jr.'s fledgling Boat Works.

Other signs pointed out the advantage of the proven Dodge engine in its marine configuration and the vast Dodge Brothers dealer network. Dodge was the first boat builder to offer the dealer advantage, and soon it was advanced by other boat-building firms. The industry acknowledged that service questions were the greatest obstacle to selling to concerned prospective owners.

Dodge, however, recognized some of his own limitations. He openly admitted that he had little desire to spend his time administering the daily operations of his own boat factory. As a result, he needed to attract competent people to important positions so that he could devote his time to racing and the other pleasures that were still more important to him. He sought staff people who possessed complete knowledge of boat construction and who fully subscribed to his straight-line production approach to boat building. He also sought to secure a well-known, professional boat builder who would provide instant name recognition. This would further demonstrate that Dodge Boat Works was on its way to becoming one of the nation's most significant boat-building firms.

Looking for a Wise Man

Armed with an abundance of personal confidence, Dodge decided to approach George Crouch to join his firm. A nationally acclaimed naval architect familiar to nearly everyone interested in powerboats and a professor at the exclusive Webb Institute in New York, Crouch was recognized as one of the brilliant designers of the time. Dodge met with Crouch and asked him to join his new company with the opportunity to run his boat factory.

As far back as 1901, Crouch was associated with the firm of Tams, Lemoine & Crane, specializing in speed and small powerboats. Crouch's first high-speed motorboat was designed and built three years before the first Gold Cup Race. From 1905 to 1923 he taught at the Webb Institute for Naval Architecture. During this same period he served as the technical editor and contributing writer for *Motor Boat* magazine. In 1910 Crouch was credited with designing the first concave, "wave capturing," V-bottom powerboat in the world. The boat, named *Peter Pan IV*, won the prestigious Hudson River Championship in its first attempt, opening the industry's eyes to Crouch's creative talent.

The Crouch runabout hull configurations influenced nearly every major runabout design for decades. In 1911 Crouch designed a 26-foot runabout called *Reliance IV* for James Simpson of New York City. Its general profile appeared similar to the typical round-bilge runabouts of that period. However, *Reliance IV* had an innovative, concave V-bottom that allowed the craft to plane smartly and reach the then-sensa-tional speed of 26 miles per hour with an engine that just produced 50 horsepower. Later the same year, the American-designed, English-built *Pioneer* came to the United States and demonstrated the advantages of the step hydroplane hull. Crouch was intrigued by the design and turned his attention to the study of the new bottom design; his step hydroplanes were among the first built in America. Crouch's three-point concept was the unique feature of *Peter Pan VIII* in 1916. Nearly each one of his early race-boat designs contributed important milestones to the advancement of the sport.

In 1913 Crouch was responsible for designing many highly successful V-bottom runabouts that could achieve speeds greater than 30 miles per hour with engines rated at less than 100 horsepower. The most prominent of these vessels were the 26-footer *Cinderella* and two 28-footers, *Marco III* and *Peter Pan Senior*. When the Sterling Engine Company of Buffalo, New York, introduced a new racing engine for hydroplanes rated at 250 horsepower, Richard Waldron of Kingston, Ontario, commissioned Crouch to design a 35-foot runabout named *Kiota III*. In its trial runs, *Kiota III* became the first runabout to achieve a speed of 40 miles per hour, then set an official American Power Boat Association (APBA) runabout record at Alexandria Bay, New York, that stood unbroken until 1919.

By 1924 some of Crouch's better-known race boats included *Rainbow IV*, *Baby Bootlegger*, and *Miss Columbia*. All three were outstanding race boats that brought even more tribute to his skill by winning first, second, and third places in the Gold Cup Regatta that year. Crouch repeated his winning streak in 1925 when *Baby Bootlegger* retained the Gold Cup against the strongest competition ever assembled up to that time. Crouch had no trouble recognizing and distinguishing the differences between boats suited for racing and those built for the pure enjoyment of comfort and speed. He became eminently skilled in the critical design elements for each style.

Crouch was well acquainted with Horace Dodge through previous dealings on his personal race boats and the development of the 22-foot *Watercar*. Crouch was impressed with Horace's concept of production line construction and enjoyed listening to his ideas about promoting greater participation in the pleasure of motorboating by making the sport more affordable. Crouch found Horace pleasant, enthusiastic, and unusually persuasive, but most of all he knew that Dodge and his family had the financial means to popularize motorboating and even influence its direction.

Dodge proposed that Crouch consider joining his new enterprise and that together they could greatly influence boating in America. The offer was certainly enticing. Crouch considered Horace's generous proposal carefully and, to the astonishment of many, agreed to leave the Webb Institute and join the Horace E. Dodge Boat Works as its new vice president.

Crouching on Success

In December 1924 the official announcement appeared in all the marine publications that Crouch's responsibilities would include engineering and production. The announcement served notice to all runabout builders that Dodge was dedicated to becoming a major force in the industry, and that with George Crouch as his key

person, he could accomplish it. The Dodge-Crouch combination presented solid respectability for the Dodge program among both boaters and competing boat builders. They reasoned that if Crouch was so moved by Dodge's concept of boat production that he would leave the Webb Institute to join him, then there had to be merit to Dodge's approach. Still, only a handful of boat builders considered adopting his concept.

In a statement to the press, Crouch said:

My principle duty, as I understand it is to see that the policy which contributed so much to the great success of Mr. Dodge's father's business, shall be applied in the strictest sense to this business. I am referring to the policy of continuous, uninterrupted improvement. We have a wonderful boat as it is, but each year brings advanced ideas and we intend to incorporate those ideas in the Watercar just as fast as we prove them to be practical and durable. I told Mr. Dodge when he first asked my opinion of the Watercar that I considered it to be one of the ablest

Horace Dodge, at left, tests one of his new race boats with designer George Crouch. At the time this rare photo capturing the two together was taken, Crouch was vice president of the Dodge Boat Works in Detroit.

The attractive new Crouch-designed 25-foot, triple-cockpit Model 826 was introduced at the 1926 National Motor Boat Show and became the second model to use the Watercar trade name. It featured the innovative rear-facing aft seat and introduced the Dodge-Curtiss V-8 engine. *William Miller*

22-footers for seaworthiness that I have ever sat in—and I believe it. The price is low and the market is growing. With the fine facilities we have for quantity production and with the superb Dodge Brothers sales organization as an outlet, I can see enormous possibilities for the Horace E. Dodge Boat Works. Otherwise, of course, I should have remained where I was.

Crouch's statement summarized the logic behind his decision to leave his faculty and his administrative responsibilities at the Webb Institute. He believed that this was a unique opportunity to advance his creative theories on marine design with the nearly unlimited resources of the Dodges Brothers auto industry behind him. Dodge now had a substantial inventory of new boats ready for delivery, a national dealer and service program, and one of the industry's most respected designers to supervise production and create new designs. Even the most skeptical observers began to admit that Dodge might be on to something big. There is no question that he had already made impressive gains in a very short time. But seasoned boat builders predicted that there still could be many stumbling blocks ahead.

For 1925, the 22-foot Watercar was still the singular standardized Dodge offering with no other models offered. Their ad for that year's National Motor Boat Show declared, "A Good Boat Made Better," and their affirmed policy of continuous improvements resulted in several

excellent enhancements. Among them was a new system for oiling and water circulation that they reported was "far superior to those found in an ordinary runabout." Standard equipment included "a self bailer to eliminate any accumulation of bilge water while underway." Dodge also pointed out that their new location at the National Motor Boat Show would be just to the left of the main entrance, another clear indication of their rising status among the show's exhibitors.

In addition to the standard display of the 1925 Watercar, Dodge brought an additional Watercar mounted very cleverly on a revolving frame that allowed the entire boat to be rotated upside down with very little effort. Using this simple device, viewers were able to examine every section of the boat conveniently and up close. This remarkably simple display technique provided one of the most interesting exhibits at the show and demonstrated Dodge's flair for innovation and his willingness to be different.

The price of the 1925 Watercar remained the same as in 1924 at $2,250, a price that its advertising copy referred to as "absurdly low." At the 1925 National Motor Boat Show, Dodge also announced the marketing of the new Dodge-Curtiss Marine Engine, a lightweight 90-horsepower V-8 with a running range of 300 to 1,600 revolutions per minute. At $1,000 complete, the Dodge-Curtiss was one of the lowest priced of any marine engine of equal power and well suited for service in speedboats.

What was most important, however, was that Crouch's appointment provided Dodge with the capability to add more standardized models and the opportunity to offer custom-built boats and special racing craft for a wider range of clients.

The Impatient Owner

In spite of abundant resources at his disposal, Horace Dodge's early racing performances had been disappointing. His boats reflected the work of excellent designers and state-of-the-art marine power. He appeared to be passionate about achieving championship recognition in racing, yet it became evident to those close to him he was talking more than he was preparing himself for success.

His goal to exceed Gar Wood's achievements and become recognized as the new speedboat king did not include dedication to rigorous preparation and long hours of practice. Horace rarely took the time to prepare either himself or his race boats properly. Each time he failed to win or to perform up to his boat's potential, he was quick to point out an unexpected problem that was beyond his control or someone else's fault as the reason for not winning. Horace often attributed his inability to win or even finish a race to "a rotten engine" or "getting cut off at the start" or "a faulty propeller." Horace never seemed willing to cite his own lack of preparation.

The 1925 Gold Cup Races were scheduled to take place on Manhasset Bay, on Long Island Sound, New York, beginning on August 29. Determined to win the prized Gold Cup, Horace entered three of his fastest race boats: *Impshi*, *Miss Syndicate*, and *Solar Plexus.* He had the boats shipped to New York by railcar and arranged for the family yacht, *Delphine*, to journey from Detroit to Long Island so that his guests and family could view the races in grand style and comfort.

The *Delphine* also carried 1,500 gallons of special high-octane fuel for his race boats to use. Horace's sister, Delphine, also decided to join her brother for the event and arranged to ship her own favorite race boat, *Nuisance,* along with a backup to Long Island, bringing the number of Dodge family entrants in the event to four. Delphine chartered a special train to ship the boats and hired a complete crew of mechanics and technicians to travel along with several guests on the train.

Full of confidence, Horace decided to drive *Solar Plexus,* but before the end of the first heat he experienced engine problems and was forced to withdraw. Of the other Dodge boats, *Impshi*, representing the Dodge Dealers Association, finished the first heat in third place.

In the second heat, *Nuisance* for eight laps made a strong bid for the lead before being forced out with a broken propeller shaft. *Impshi*, with Colonel Jesse Vincent of Packard Motors at the wheel, finished the heat just three seconds out of first place. All hope for a Dodge victory vanished when *Impshi* was unable to start for the third heat. In a strange irony, the winning boat at the 1925 Gold Cup was Caleb Bragg's *Baby Bootlegger*, designed by Dodge's new vice president, George Crouch. The paradox of the Crouch victory and the praise for his new vice president didn't go unnoticed by Dodge.

To add insult to injury, *Delphine* sustained hull damage on the trip to Long Island; all during the races her pumps had to run continuously just to keep the big yacht afloat. Immediately after the races, *Delphine* went into dry dock for hull repairs. When the repairs were completed, Horace's mother returned to New York with guests to cruise on the Hudson River before the yacht made its return trip to Detroit. While still at anchor in New York, Anna and her guests disembarked to attend the New York Opera. Upon their return they found that the *Delphine* had caught fire, and the misdirected attempt to extinguish the blaze flooded the hull, sinking the yacht just a few feet from the dock. It was an incredible disaster, but Anna was not about to let her late husband's grand yacht be lost in such a disgraceful manner. She empowered her captain to make all the arrangements necessary to have the hull raised and to supervise the yacht's full restoration to original condition.

Flirting with Distraction
During the early winter, Horace left Lois and the children behind while he traveled to Europe, ostensibly, on a business trip. The rumor traveling around Detroit was that he was infatuated with Muriel Sisman, the daughter of a successful Detroit developer and a debutante whom he had met at the Night in Venice party that Lois had organized three years earlier.

When the rumor finally reached Anna Dodge, she contacted her son insisting that he return to Detroit at once. While he was still en route, Lois was involved in a serious automobile accident on December 26 in which a friend of Lois was killed. Anna hoped that this tragic accident would bring Horace to his senses and that Lois' injuries would draw them closer together.

When her recovery was complete, Lois expressed greater interest in Horace's boat activities and made every effort to do what she could to mend their marriage. She even encouraged him to open a sales office in Palm Beach to promote the new boats. The effort was sincere but soon abandoned.

With its stately long deck, the early Watercar provided a rather dignified image, with a large, comfortable, and socially congenial cockpit that many boat owners preferred. By 1927, however, its conservative style was becoming outmoded. *Lindsey Hopkins III*

Chapter Four

Introducing the Watercar

With his enormous financial position, Horace Dodge was off to an impressive start. He had

employed creative concepts, offered an attractive boat, hired a well-known and respected

designer, and taken advantage of an existing brand reputation and dealer organization. Dodge

also announced that the volume planned for their first full year of production would exceed

the output that any boat builder had ever attained. Dodge ads were well crafted and served

notice to buyers and boat builders alike that there was an exciting new kid on the block.

Following their highly successful debut at the 1924 National Motor Boat Show, Dodge

Watercar promotions began stressing the two brand names in bold print along with three

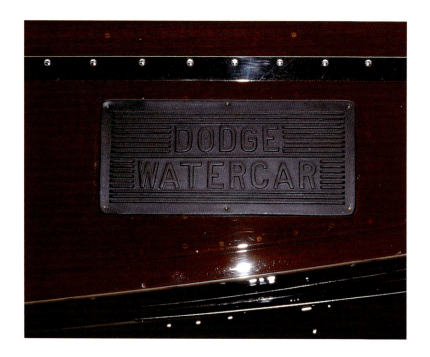

The original rectangular "Dodge Watercar" black rubber step pad was used on all Dodge boat models through 1929, before it was replaced in 1930 by the more attractive white rubber oval design.

Right: Calypso is one of the first of 111 22-foot, 2-inch Watercars built by Martin Draeger's straight-line production team at the Racine Manufacturing Company. *Marty Loken*

key facts for readers to remember: (1) The boats and the engines were products of large-quantity production; (2) Dodge service stations were located throughout the country; and (3) All Dodge auto dealers provided their national sales distribution information.

Horace Dodge hit the boat market with everything he had, and it appeared that he was leading simultaneous revolutions in standardized

boat building and creative marketing. Having quickly captured the attention of boat buyers, other boat builders began to think that Horace might be on to something.

Cracks Appear in Horace's Plans

Chris Smith and his sons Jay and Bernard in nearby Algonac, Michigan, knew that Dodge was on the right track with standardized design and production lines and became advocates of this type of building to increase efficiency and reduce costs. They also believed in the development of a strong dealer network modeled after car dealers. However, they felt that young Dodge might be moving too fast.

Chris Smith thought that while using automobile dealers to sell boats sounded very clever, boats and cars presented very different challenges. A good location for an auto dealer, for example, might be a totally inappropriate location to service the needs of boat owners. The Smiths planned to watch Dodge carefully and see how things developed for his Watercar concept. They were already into standardization with their runabouts and were establishing procedures to take advantage of production line technology. With Dodge moving quickly in this direction, they could study his progress and learn from his experiences.

With 1924 production subcontracted to the Racine Manufacturing Company and an abundant supply of boats stored in his new factory in Detroit, Dodge soon learned that all his enthusiastic talk about production line efficiency was far easier than the constant requirements of keeping those lines running. Although he struck an interesting deal with Dodge Brothers automobile dealers, very few were ready to order a boat for stock. They were more amenable to distributing boat brochures to inquiring customers and taking orders if one of their customers was ready to purchase a Watercar.

The dealers were extremely cautious about becoming too involved too quickly. After all, the business of selling and servicing automobiles was still in its infancy; most automobile dealers were hard-pressed to keep up with the demands of automobile customers let alone devoting time and space to selling boats. In the minds of most car dealers, boats and automobiles didn't seem to be as natural a combination as Horace had believed.

Adding Substance to Reality

Hired in December 1924 as Dodge's vice president of engineering and production, George

Crouch knew immediately that Dodge's production line boat-building concept would only work properly if a powerful marketing and sales program was firmly in place to absorb the factory output. The key to this approach was to seek and appoint dedicated marine dealers with the facilities to handle boats and their service. While the concept of selling boats through Dodge auto dealers made for excellent publicity, it was

Above: The original 22-foot long-deck Watercars that debuted in 1924 and remained in production through 1927 were attractive, smooth handling, and soft riding. *Lindsey Hopkins III*

The attractive combination navigation light in gleaming brass on the 22-foot Watercar holds the burgee staff over the attractive African mahogany deck. *Lindsey Hopkins III*

more fluff than substance. What Dodge needed was a network of dealers who would actively stock, promote, sell, and service his boats.

Crouch insisted that Dodge Boat Works needed to focus its sales efforts in regions where boating was already popular. He also felt that in order to attract serious dealers it was necessary to expand the Watercar lineup. In his opinion, the original 22-foot model was a good boat, but too conservative. Boating trends were changing quickly and runabouts with cockpits and controls forward of the engine were becoming the rage. Crouch insisted that the key to mass production manufacturing was the development of reliable high-volume sales.

Dodge agreed and at the 1926 National Motor Boat Show unveiled a new Watercar, a 26-foot, triple-cockpit runabout identified as the Model 826, the second Dodge boat to carry the Watercar designation. The new Crouch-designed

Dodge purchased large quantities of World War I–surplus Curtiss OX aircraft engines, converting them for marine use in 22- and 26-foot runabouts from 1926 to 1928. *Robert Weaver*

runabout was a stunning craft with a unique rear-facing seat in a large aft cockpit. The unusual position of the seat provided additional space for chairs or cargo, and the beam at 6 feet, 7 inches was generous for the time, giving the boat an attractive, modern appearance. Dodge brochures claimed that there was enough room in the forward twin cockpits for seven passengers and that another five or six could fit in the generous aft cockpit.

The 826 was offered at $3,475 with the new Dodge-Curtiss V-8 rated at 90 to 100 horsepower and providing a top speed of 35 miles per hour. A lot of people agreed that this model was one of the best values in a quality runabout. (The same boat was offered with the 30-horsepower Dodge four-cylinder engine. Rated at 17 miles per hour, the underpowered Model 426 was an attempt to satisfy Dodge's continued desire to offer boats at a more moderate price.)

Crouch had also insisted that some modifications be made to the original 22-foot Watercar. The redesignated Model 422 retained the 30-horsepower Dodge four-cylinder, but the hull was increased in length to 22 feet, 6 inches. A high-performance version, powered with the Dodge-Curtiss engine, was called the Model 822 and could attain the speed of 37 miles per hour. The additional power increased the price by $570 and opened a broader market for the established design.

Expanding the Lineup

In the fall, Dodge Boat Works acquired a factory more suitable for their style of production on Lycaste Avenue with access to the Detroit River for in-water testing. The former East Atwater Street factory was used for storage of new boats ready to be shipped to dealers, as well as producing one-of-a-kind custom boats and Horace's race boats.

George Crouch was also well aware of the interest created by big runabouts, such as Gar Wood's 33-foot Baby Gars, among wealthy sportsmen and felt that Dodge should attempt to reach out to those who wanted an impressive runabout without going to the extreme size and power of a Baby Gar. His answer was the Model 630, an attractive flush-deck, triple-cockpit 30-foot runabout with very modern lines. Powered with a dependable 250-horsepower Globe engine

George Crouch designed the impressive 37-foot *Horace* for Horace Jr., with a variety of purposes in mind, including commuter, yacht tender, and race boat. Powered with a Wright-Typhoon 650-horsepower engine, it was capable of speeds in the range of 60 miles per hour. The massive boat has been well preserved and still uses its original Wright-Typhoon powerplant.

providing speeds over 40 miles per hour, one of its interesting features was a very large aft cockpit with two rows of seats facing each other. Dodge's promotional description stated that the Model 630's production for 1927 would be limited to 25 units, several of which had already been ordered. It was clearly the most elegant standard runabout from any builder and capable of carrying 14 passengers in comfort. The big runabout was identified as the Watercar Senior and offered at $7,200. It took three more years before Gar Wood brought out a competitive modern, flush-deck 30-plus-foot runabout.

It was becoming more evident that building boats that were within reach of average working families was losing ground as Dodge's prime objective. At the time, the average three-bedroom home in America cost $4,500, and the typical two-door Dodge sedan sold for less than $900. With the average American's annual income around $1,600, how could a working family afford $2,475 for a new Watercar? To Crouch it made more sense to secure the business, establish dependable sales agencies, refine the methods of production, and then offer a modestly priced boat. For the moment, at least,

Horace, the versatile, high-performance racing runabout was eligible for the 150-mile Sweepstakes Race and the Gold Cup. It was given a "D" designation that assigned it to the Developmental Class.

Dodge was so preoccupied with his faltering marriage that he was agreeable to the need for models with stronger appeal and gave his approval for the additional new Watercars. Then he began making plans for a business trip to Europe, a pretense to pursue the charming Muriel Sisman.

After Horace announced the trip, the chances of Lois and Horace reconciling their marital problems appeared to be less likely, and Lois filed for divorce in 1927. On January 20, a press release appeared in several major newspapers stating:

Horace E. Dodge, President of the Horace E. Dodge Boat Works of Detroit and son of the late manufacturer of Dodge Brothers motor cars, left this week for Europe. He will make a first hand study of every important boat building plant in England and on the Continent. He will be gone from three to six months. In traveling about from city to city, he will use his own Stinson airplane, piloted by his personal

aviator, Marion Sterling. Mr. Sterling is following Mr. Dodge with the plane in about two weeks and will meet him in Paris whence they will start out on their tour of the boat building plants with the idea of adapting any new manufacturing ideas, if any, to the construction of the four models of standardized Dodge Watercars now being built in Detroit.

Reporters in Europe had no problem catching up with Horace at the gambling tables in Cannes. By his side throughout each interview was his new love, Muriel Sisman. In May the divorce was settled. Lois' attorney based her claim on the grounds that "her husband's interest in speedboats kept him away from home and made her unhappy. He had violent temper spells, would go away and stay away for weeks at a time."

By the time the divorce was finalized, the styling features for the three 1927 Dodge models were ready. The new Crouch models were well received and Dodge was confident that they were moving in the right direction. He also was sure

Two Watercars outside Dodge's Lycaste Avenue factory in 1927, ready for shipment in response to an urgent telegraph from the Mississippi Red Cross ordering a single 22-foot Watercar to aid flood victims. Dodge responded immediately, shipping the boat that was ordered, along with a new 26-foot Watercar that he donated to aid the organization's efforts.

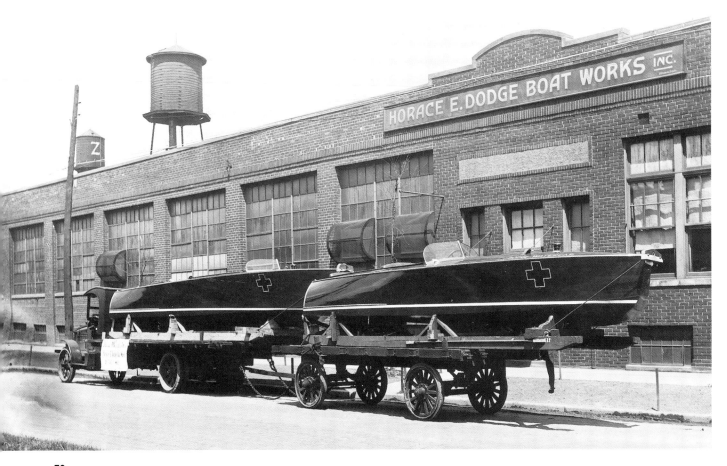

that it would be the final production year for the original 22-footer. He was so impressed with the new 30-foot Model 630 that he asked Crouch to design a bigger version of the splendid craft for his personal use.

One of Crouch's special designs for his new boss was the 37-foot mahogany *Horace*, a magnificent runabout with three generous cockpits and powered by a 12-cylinder Wright-Typhoon engine rated at 650 horsepower. The engine, built by the Wright Aeronautical Corporation, was located just aft of midships and provided *Horace* with sustained speeds in the range of 60 miles per hour. It was designed to provide its owner with a fast, comfortable yacht tender that was also capable of racing for the Gold Cup, 150-mile Sweepstakes, or the President's Cup. It won the Championship of the Potomac and placed second to one of the most extreme race craft ever built in the President's Cup Race. Displacing 9,000 pounds, the husky *Horace* operated with great ease in the roughest water conditions.

Staging a Publicity Coup

Horace wanted to do something spectacular for the next boat show issues of the major boating magazines, so he contacted each one of the Watercar's major suppliers to get them to participate in a massive advertisement that covered 30 consecutive pages. The banner across the top of each page would feature the words "Dodge Watercars" printed boldly across the page. Between the two words would appear an image of the fabulous $15,000 Dodge Memorial Trophy. The rest of each page would be devoted to the suppliers' advertising copy explaining their connection, of course, with Dodge Boat Works.

To encourage full participation from his suppliers, Dodge negotiated a significant discount from each magazine. His power of persuasion and creativity was at its best and the impact of the 30-page ad was very powerful. Suppliers of propellers, engines, fastenings, paints, varnishes, upholstery, nickel plating, electric power tools, fuel filters, dash instruments, and propeller shafts all joined this special promotion. It was so impressive that Horace reproduced the entire segment as a self-contained brochure for his dealers to distribute.

Horace affected another publicity coup that year when heavy rains forced the Mississippi River

to overflow its bank and the Clarksdale Mississippi Division of the Red Cross placed a rush order by telegraph for a 22-foot Dodge Watercar to aid in emergency rescue work. Horace Dodge filled the order within hours of receiving the request and even donated an additional 26-foot Watercar to assist the cause. Large Red Cross logos were painted on the hull sides, and both boats were rushed by truck and trailer to Clarksdale.

Reports that followed said that the Watercars performed superbly and at times were the only craft that could operate against the rushing water. The Red Cross report concluded by stating, "The Dodge Watercars ran from 200 to 300 miles per day carrying medical supplies to flood victims and rescuing hundreds of people from house tops and crumbling levees without a single breakdown."

Marine reporter George Sutton interviewed Dodge in 1927 for a feature story in *Motor Boating* magazine. Entitled "Why We Are Leading a Boat Revolution," the story gave Horace another grand opportunity to present his position to the boating world. He wasted no time and was quoted stating:

> There is no valid reason why the manufacture of motorboats should not have been conducted in the same efficient and progressive manner as millions of motor cars. Dodge Watercars are produced in much the same manner as finer automobiles such as Packard, Pierce-Arrow, Lincoln, Cadillac and others.
>
> Gradually the thought was forced upon me—can the standardization methods of

This candid photograph from a Red Cross worker was sent to Horace Dodge and shows his donated 26-foot Watercar transporting flood victims in Mississippi. The two Watercars often covered 150 or more miles a day, carrying medical supplies and food for needy flood victims.

A 1929 26-foot Watercar Sedan runabout waits to be loaded for overseas delivery to the Spanish sportswoman, Señora Maria Pelayo.

automobile manufacturing be successfully applied to boat building? The answer is, as we know now, that they can be so applied and could have been adopted by boat makers back in 1902. From the remarkable results that we have obtained in a few short years, the Dodge Boat Works as presently constituted, represents the manner in which the whole motorboat industry of the future must operate to supply the public with reliable, economical, well-built, standardized boats.

Taking on the Speedboat King

With his divorce from Lois settled, Horace turned his attention to the upcoming Labor Day Sweepstakes races in the Detroit River, confident that this would be the race in which he could successfully challenge Gar Wood and win.

Horace had two boats ready and felt that either *Solar Plexus* or *Miss Syndicate* could beat Wood's *Baby Gar VIII*. Horace began bragging that the time was right for him and even made the audacious statement that "Gar Wood doesn't know how to build a boat." He continued by saying, "Wood may be able to drive and he may know motors, but he can't put speed into a hull."

As it turned out, Wood had to sit out the race because he was injured just four days prior when he was thrown from a boat in a practice run. Wood sent his boat, *Baby Gar VIII*, with an

In this composite photograph, Horace Dodge Jr. "poses" in front of his Stinson biplane on January 19, 1927, prior to one of his "boat building" trips to England. In reality, it was a front to pursue Muriel Sisman, soon to become his second wife.

alternate crew to enter the race in his place. Horace selected *Miss Syndicate* and drove to victory. As Herbert Stone reported in *Yachting*, "It was a well-deserved victory in a major event after years of heartbreaking disappointment and hard luck, during which Dodge spent a fortune in the development of fast boats." Dodge's other entry, *Solar Plexus*, finished second, and Wood's boat, *Baby Gar VIII*, finished third. The win was a bit disappointing because Horace didn't have the chance to beat the "speedboat king" himself.

Still, after his Sweepstakes victory, Horace felt more confident than ever. He was never shy, but now he was even more apt to take a shot or two at Gar Wood whenever he had a chance. The popular *Detroit News* sportswriter Harry Leduc reported in his column that Dodge "seldom missed an opportunity to discuss the greatness of Wood. Never failing to remark that he always welcomed the opportunity of racing against him and would even welcome a match race between himself and Wood in any class of boat the two happened to own." Leduc quoted Dodge directly when he stated: "Wood hasn't built a winner since he quit the Smiths. I'll beat him the first time we meet."

In September 1927 Horace was determined to make one more try at the 150-mile National

Top: Designed in 1925 by George Crouch for Horace Jr., the 25-foot Gold Cup racer *Solar Plexus* finished fourth in the 1926 Gold Cup and won the 1927 Developmental Class Race. It became one of Dodge's most enduring race boats, winning the 1932 Gold Cup Race with Bill Horn driving it under its new name, *Delphine IV.*

Above: In the 1927 Sweepstakes Race, the boastful and confident Horace Dodge Jr. challenged Gar Wood's experimental Gold Cup racer, *Baby Gar VIII*. Wood, injured a few days before the race, sent a substitute driver who finished third. Dodge won.

Sweepstakes Race. To improve his chances, he prepared four Dodge boats for the important event. He would drive the two-year-old, Crouch-designed *Miss Syndicate.* The other Dodge entries would include *Solar Plexus, Sister Syn,* and *Bottoms Up.* The water was smooth for the long event with only three other entries. Horace drove a flawless race and avoided unnecessary risks, averaging just over 47 miles per hour. The victory was sweet, and *Motor Boat* magazine reported, "Horace Dodge has finally succeeded in his ambition to win the Sweepstakes, a prize that he has been after for several years. At times it has been almost in his grasp, only to be lost by mechanical failures and mishaps."

A Parting of the Ways

It was becoming apparent to George Crouch that Horace Dodge was better as a client than he was as a business associate or employer. Horace's most apparent skill seemed to be his ability to convince others with charm and enthusiasm when it suited him. He clearly lacked the motivation and desire to stay on task and do all that was necessary to achieve any stated goal. His boat-building venture had merit and could succeed as a viable business venture if he was willing to remain diligent to the task, but Horace

constantly allowed distractions to dominate his attention. This lack of dedication coupled with his angry outbursts did not sit well with his staff.

Crouch recognized that his best interest was to move on. His reputation was as yet unblemished and his design skills were well established—he was ready to test his ability to survive on his own as an independent naval architect. When he informed Horace of his decision in late summer 1927, it was met without acrimony. As an independent contractor, Crouch continued designing race boats for Dodge and was available as a consultant. His role as vice president of the Horace E. Dodge Boat Works concluded quietly without any apparent animosity. Shortly after Crouch left, Horace was involved in a messy lawsuit against a syndicate that revealed the growing financial problems at Dodge Boat Works. Horace had invested heavily to purchase and develop of more than 1,000 acres of land in Michigan's Oakland County. Dodge's attorney claimed that he had been influenced "by high powered sales talk" into giving the syndicate organizer $120,000 in notes that, instead, were then used to pay off the defendant's personal debts. Unsympathetically, the judge asked

Dodge's attorney if his client was "sane and sober when he gave all this money without a receipt?" Then, on the witness stand, the defendant made the embarrassing revelation that Dodge not only was eager to invest in the land development syndicate, but he wanted help to refinance his insolvent Boat Works, which was becoming strapped for cash.

Over the course of the lawsuit, Horace's embarrassment increased and he left Detroit for England with his two children; it was one of the ways he had learned to handle uncomfortable situations. When he arrived in London, he announced plans to marry Muriel Sisman in early May 1928, one year after his divorce from Lois.

Top: The 32-foot Gold Cup racer *Sister Syn* was designed by George Crouch and built in 1925 for Horace Jr.'s sister, Delphine Dodge Cromwell. Here, the boat is ready to go at the 2002 Race Boat Regatta in Clayton, New York.

Inset: *Sister Syn*'s magnificent 12-cylinder, 650-horsepower Curtiss Conqueror engine is an impressive source of power.

While still in England, Horace settled the land investment lawsuit out of court and made plans to take up residence in England. Anna and her new husband, Hugh Dillman, with whom she made frequent trips abroad, returned to America with Horace's two children, furious over Horace's disinterest in returning to Dodge Boat Works, which was falling into serious financial trouble and had yet to show a profit.

Anna's Ultimatum

Anna contacted her son in England and insisted that he return to manage the operation, even threatened to close it down. Somehow, her ultimatum reached the press, and newspapers reported, "Mrs. Dillman Closes Dodge Boat Works." After a flurry of cablegrams between Anna and Horace, a statement was issued to the press stating that the Atwater Street plant had only been closed for the long Labor Day weekend and that the cutbacks in their labor force was their traditional season layoff.

In April 1928 an editorial announcement appeared in *Power Boating* magazine stating:

> Horace E. Dodge of Detroit, president of the boat building company that bears his name, has announced a number of changes in his organization. He is now taking over the active management of the company personally. He has appointed the following men as his assistants: William Horn, an amateur race boat driver and mechanician whose experience in boat racing covered a decade or more; William "Billy" Martin who recently drove a 26-foot Chrysler powered Watercar from Detroit to Miami in a well-publicized media event. Martin was schooled in automobile production; and Harry E. Chapman who has been with Dodge since 1923. Chapman had a strong background in automobile production, merchandising and body manufacturing.

Dodge established a goal of building 600 new boats in 1928. After three and a half years of production, the original 22-foot Watercar, with its conservative, launch-style appearance, was to be discontinued and replaced. Its appearance had become dated by several contemporary runabout designs and the cost of its construction kept it beyond the reach of its intended buyers. In its place, Dodge introduced a new model identified as the "Sport-A-Bout" at the low price of $1,595. The 20-footer was claimed to be the consummate "plain Jane" of runabouts.

With Crouch gone, Dodge resumed his original goal of providing an affordable boat for the working family. To keep the cost as low as possible, the Sport-A-Bout was offered with a painted hull and painted decks. To make the cost-saving feature appear more attractive, Dodge gave each of the three hull color schemes enticing

The 1928 Sport-A-Bout was an interesting but short-lived experiment to create a less-expensive, attractively painted model with little hardware and no windshields. At just $1,595, it replaced the 22-foot Watercar.

names such as *Polly Green*, *Lady Mary Maroon*, and *Coach Black*. All three featured black decks. The absence of traditional hardware and trim was another attempt to keep the cost of the boat as modest as possible.

Standard Sport-A-Bout models left the factory devoid of windshields, deck ventilators, lifting rings, fender cleats, chocks, and cutwaters. The boat was designed with two cockpits, one forward and one aft of the engine compartment with seating for six. The only power offered was the venerable 30-horsepower Dodge Brothers four-cylinder, which when coupled with the Sport-A-Bout hull provided modest speeds of around 22 miles per hour.

The Sport-A-Bout was promoted frequently throughout 1928, but its sales were disappointing. Dodge decided that the market wasn't ready for the "plain Jane" craft, and his managers convinced him to discontinue it. Dodge's young staff

designer, Walt Leveau, quickly went to work to transform the 20-footer into a more respectable runabout by making a few practical changes, beginning with a varnished finish and a bright cutwater for the African mahogany hull. The boat was equipped with a normal complement of deck hardware, including dual sets of windshields. The revamped 1929 model was dubbed simply the "Runabout" and priced at $1,675, just $80 more than the Sport-A-Bout. To provide greater speed, an optional six-cylinder engine that raised speeds to 30 miles per hour was offered for an additional $425. Not surprisingly, this attractive twin-windshield runabout proved to be more popular than the brightly painted Sport-A-Bout.

The 14-page Dodge Watercar sales brochure for 1929 devoted the majority of its pages and text to the reestablishment of its proud Dodge name and their auto and yachting heritage. There was no question that concern for the

In 1929 Dodge Boat Works transformed the 20-foot Sport-A-Bout into a runabout by varnishing the hull and adding twin windshields and trim. The result was this split-cockpit runabout. *Lindsey Hopkins III*

Dodge's price leader in 1928 and 1929 was the 20-foot split-cockpit runabout, an attractive and nicely proportioned model demonstrating that Dodge was moving toward modern styling ahead of their rivals. *Marty Loken*

Dodge favored automobile-style dash panels and located steering columns on the left, as observed in this 20-foot 1928 runabout. *Marty Loken*

future existence of Dodge Boat Works was raised every time another negative report surfaced. The buzz about Dodge in boating circles began with George Crouch's rather brief stay with the company. Rumors were fueled by Horace's absence from the factory, his apparent lack of leadership, Anna's questionable decision to briefly close the Boat Works, and the emphasis on building "affordable" boats that were actually beyond the reach of working families.

Perhaps the biggest disappointment, however, was the failed concept of using Dodge automobile dealers as a national sales and service network. It turned out to be a ploy that lacked the serious dedication necessary to make it work properly. All of these concerns gradually began to erode the confidence of potential buyers. It was about this time when the Atwater Street office staff began to refer to their absentee owner as "H.E." in reference to Dodge's first and middle initials. The nickname stuck and was used throughout the factory, although never to address Horace Elgin directly.

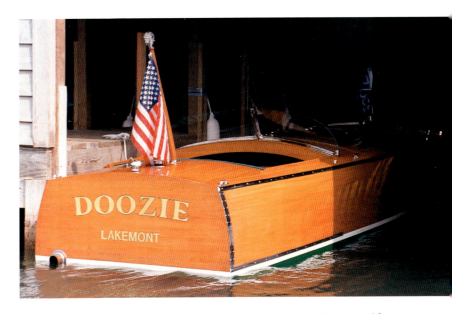

Doozie is a rare surviving example of Dodge's 1929 20-foot runabout that emerged from a major upgrade of the original Sport-A-Bout. A varnished hull, twin windshields, and bright cutwater and trim raised the price by just $80. *Lindsey Hopkins III*

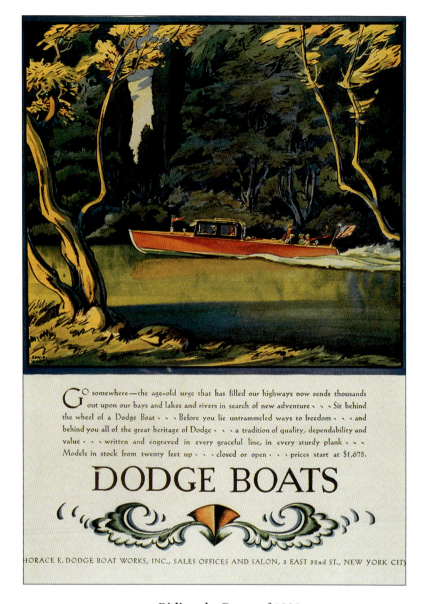

Go somewhere—the age-old urge that has filled our highways now sends thousands out upon our bays and lakes and rivers in search of new adventure ، ، ، Sit behind the wheel of a Dodge Boat ، ، ، Before you lie untrammeled ways to freedom ، ، ، and behind you all of the great heritage of Dodge ، ، ، a tradition of quality, dependability and value ، ، ، written and engraved in every graceful line, in every sturdy plank ، ، ، Models in stock from twenty feet up ، ، ، closed or open ، ، ، prices start at $1,675.

DODGE BOATS

HORACE E. DODGE BOAT WORKS, INC., SALES OFFICES AND SALON, 3 EAST 52nd ST., NEW YORK CITY

Watercar Senior buyers also were given the option of a sedan cabin version as depicted in this Edward Wilson advertisement. The slightly slower boat, also powered by the 250-horsepower Globe engine, offered speeds from 36 to 41 miles per hour.

Riding the Boom of 1929

Dodge's three standardized runabouts, the 20-, 26-, and 30-foot models, sold well in spite of the constant absenteeism of their president, now living in England, and the continued reports of uncertainty that dogged the firm. Horace's mother made a monumental effort to lure Horace back to the States and take charge of his boat business once more. Anna promised her son that if he returned she would back his ambitions, such as they were, with millions of dollars. In the booming economy of 1929, Horace decided to squeeze every bit of financial support that he could from Anna. He insisted on forming a new company in a new location that would also build aircraft. The new venture would be known as the Horace E. Dodge Boat

and Plane Corporation. Horace, of course, would be its president, and the Dodge family would retain all corporate stock.

Perhaps the greatest surprise that Horace pulled was revealing that he would acquire 100 acres of waterfront land in Newport News, Virginia, to construct his new state-of-the-art factory. His plan was to produce a line of entirely new boats and small amphibious seaplanes. He wanted it to be the world's largest factory devoted to the construction of pleasure boats. Its location on the shore of Chesapeake Bay, where the weather would not be a factor for most of the year, was an ideal site to test its products.

Moving quickly, construction of the factory, boathouses, railroad sidings, landing field, and storage sheds began in early September 1929. As soon as the construction was complete, Horace promised that he would return from England to run the new operation with its anticipated staff of 2,000 employees.

The 1929 Dodge sales brochure contains a lengthy essay that provides the reader with the story of the incredible success of the Dodge brothers, John and Horace Sr., producing high-quality automobiles at modest prices. It continues by describing their love for fine boats and includes photographs of the 52-foot *Lotus* in 1896, the 93-foot *Hornet* in 1903, the 247-foot *Nakomis II* in 1917, and the magnificent 257-foot *Delphine* launched in 1921. Each of these remarkable yachts was designed or influenced by the genius of the Dodge brothers.

The brochure stated, "Such is the background of the Dodge Boats of today; such that the ancestry from which they are the worthy descendents. Such is the tradition, which is not only a source of inspiration and practical experience, but an almost sacred obligation upon the Dodge organization of today. It is a tradition of which each Dodge boat must be worthy."

The brochure went on to point out that *Miss Syndicate*, *Horace*, and *Sister Syn* were perhaps the most famous speed craft developed by Dodge designers and were conclusive proof of their staunchness. "Dodge Motorboats are the root from which is destined to grow an industry that will produce, as Detroit genius has already produced, thousands of trans-

Dodge runabouts, like this 20-foot example from the 1928 and 1929 lineup, seemed to provide more generous aft-cockpit space than competitors' models. *Marty Loken*

ASECRET OF CHARM is its elusiveness ～ ～ ～ What makes man love boats is as hard to define as what makes the silvered waters of lake and bay so romantic and alluring ～ ～ ～ What makes those who love boats prefer Dodge Boats is easier to understand ～ ～ ～ Now, as always, the Dodge name stands for worth and quality too deep and fine to be imprisoned in cold type ～ ～ ～ All the wealth of motor lore inherent in the honored name of Dodge is manifest in every detail of the boats themselves ～ ～ ～ Models in stock from twenty feet up, closed or open. Prices start at $1,675 ～ ～ ～

DODGE BOATS

HORACE E. DODGE BOAT WORKS, INC., SALES OFFICES AND SALON, 3 EAST 52nd ST., NEW YORK CITY

Art Surpasses Life

As Horace's great expansion plans took shape, he again reached back to his automobile roots, where artists were often employed to create exciting illustrations to attract potential buyers. He contacted the well-known artist and illustrator Edward A. Wilson to create a distinctive and attractive advertising program. At that time, skilled artists could create illustrations that would stimulate even more interest than traditional photography. The plan would bring full color to Horace Dodge's ads and give his boats a decided edge over the competition. It was an extraordinary idea that reestablished Dodge as an innovative force in the boat industry.

Edward A. Wilson's art was both creative and accurate and provided proper detail and proportion to the Dodge boats in imaginative settings. During his career Wilson illustrated more than 70 books, including editions of such popular titles as *Two Years Before the Mast*, *Treasure Island*, *Around the World in Eighty Days*, *Robinson Crusoe*, *Last of the Mohicans*, and *The Journey to the Center of the Earth*. By 1929 he was a leading illustrator in high demand and received numerous awards and recognition for his work. He was the perfect choice for Dodge and began preparing a series of inspired paintings of Dodge boats that began appearing in several important periodicals.

In its open-runabout version, the 30-foot 1926 to 1928 Watercar Senior reached speeds of 40 to 45 miles per hour with a 250-horsepower Globe engine. Edward Wilson evocatively captured that sense of speed and power in this print ad, one of several he executed for Dodge.

portation units at a price that can put a motorboat within reach of almost everyone who loves the great outdoors."

It was also in this 1929 brochure that the first indication of Horace Dodge's plan to build a new factory was publicly disclosed. "Another chapter in the history of Dodge achievement and service is now being written. The present Dodge factory is already too small to house and hold the Dodge tradition. New facilities are planned for building more Dodge Motorboats including cruisers and any type of boat built to individual specifications. Thus the Dodge ideal is on its way to realization on a still greater scale."

This remarkable photograph shows *Baby Horace III* as it was discovered in 1984 after decades in storage in a Dodge family warehouse. It has since been totally restored. *Thomas Mittler*

It was Horace's plan that each month there would appear a different Wilson illustration of a Dodge boat. His work was a blend of accurate interpretation and detail of the particular boat, which was embellished with an eye-catching and attractive setting. It was a powerful combination that worked superbly. Each layout was planned to occupy a full page with Wilson's colorful illustrations as the dominant features. The ads appeared in all major boating magazines as well as periodicals that appealed to sportsmen, travelers, and financial investors.

Right: Another Edward Wilson ad shows the Dodge Runabout built from 1930 to 1934. The ad trumpets the comparative value Dodge boats represented.

Below: Baby Horace III, Dodge's 1924 Sweepstakes racer that set a displacement class speed record of 60.3 miles per hour, gets a little "exercise." *Thomas Mittler*

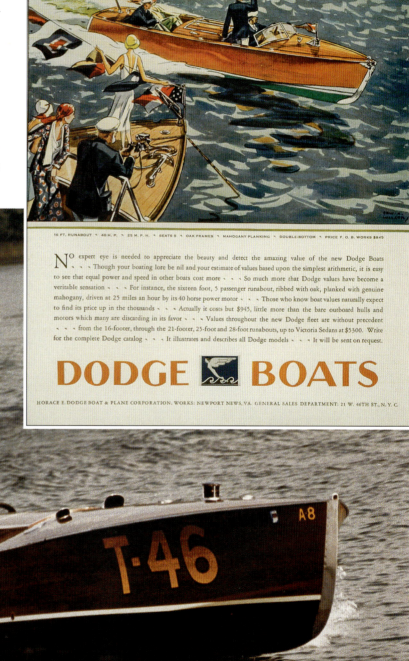

16 FT. RUNABOUT ✦ 40 H.P. ✦ 25 M.P.H. ✦ SEATS 5 ✦ OAK FRAMES ✦ MAHOGANY PLANKING ✦ DOUBLE-BOTTOM ✦ PRICE F.O.B. WORKS $945

No expert eye is needed to appreciate the beauty and detect the amazing value of the new Dodge Boats ✦ ✦ ✦ Though your boating lore be nil and your estimate of values based upon the simplest arithmetic, it is easy to see that equal power and speed in other boats cost more ✦ ✦ ✦ So much more that Dodge values have become a veritable sensation ✦ ✦ ✦ For instance, the sixteen foot, 5 passenger runabout, ribbed with oak, planked with genuine mahogany, driven at 25 miles an hour by its 40 horse power motor ✦ ✦ ✦ Those who know boat values naturally expect to find its price up in the thousands ✦ ✦ ✦ Actually it costs but $945, little more than the bare outboard hulls and motors which many are discarding in its favor ✦ ✦ ✦ Values throughout the new Dodge fleet are without precedent ✦ ✦ ✦ from the 16-footer, through the 21-footer, 25-foot and 28-foot runabouts, up to Victoria Sedans at $5300. Write for the complete Dodge catalog ✦ ✦ ✦ It illustrates and describes all Dodge models ✦ ✦ ✦ It will be sent on request.

DODGE BOATS

HORACE E. DODGE BOAT & PLANE CORPORATION. WORKS: NEWPORT NEWS, VA. GENERAL SALES DEPARTMENT: 21 W. 46TH ST., N.Y.C.

The proposed interior floor plan of the Newport News factory was released in 1929 showing each production department and the locations of manufacturing support service areas.

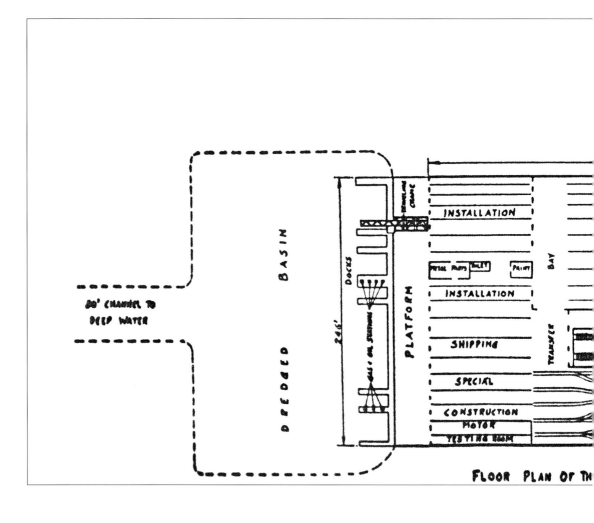

FLOOR PLAN OF TH

Thirty Dodge paintings were prepared for this special advertising campaign that lasted nearly three years. The Wilson illustrations were extremely well received and became regular items of interest that readers anticipated. Proof of the ads' value to Dodge became apparent when one of Wilson's Dodge boat illustrations received an award for artistic excellence at the 1930 Art Exhibition in New York City. It was another example of Horace's creative potential at its best. Wilson's Dodge boat ads are still sought by collectors of marine art 70 years later.

Wall Street Crashes

Construction of the new factory in Newport News was fully underway when the stock market crashed on October 29, 1929. At the time, few people understood the far-reaching impact that the event might have on the economy. Prosperity had been so widespread that it was hard to imagine the prolonged financial crisis that loomed ahead. Nonetheless, work on the new factory continued as Anna and Hugh traveled aboard a ship around the world in search of rare antiques.

Horace, meanwhile, was in England planning to return to the States as the construction in Virginia neared completion. Although the crash would have little effect on him personally, his long-held dream of manufacturing boats for average working families had received a fatal setback.

Right: The prototype for Dodge's 1930 25-foot runabout is shown with neither its side-wing windshield nor its Sea Nymph during trial runs in Detroit. The Newport News factory was under construction at the time.

*Plan of the Horace
E. Dodge plant
showing how the
units are located*

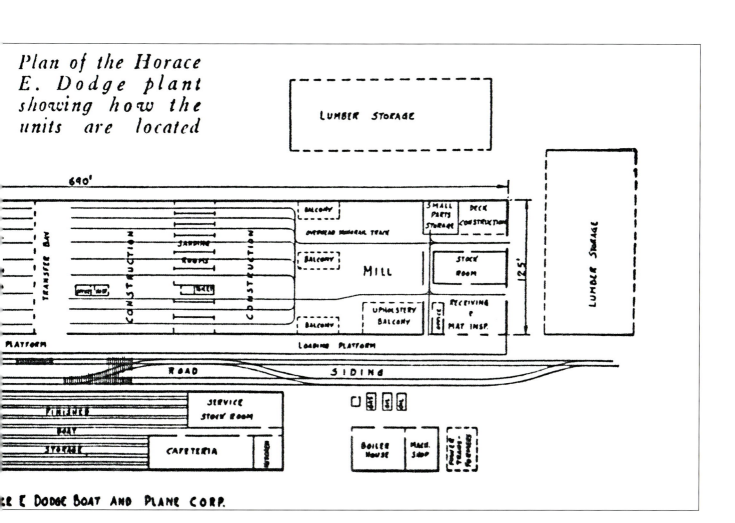

LUMBER STORAGE

690'

TRANSFER BAY

CONSTRUCTION

SANDING ROOMS

CONSTRUCTION

BALCONY

OVERHEAD MONORAIL TRACK

BALCONY

MILL

UPHOLSTERY BALCONY

BALCONY

SMALL PARTS STORAGE

DECK CONSTRUCTION

STOCK ROOM

RECEIVING & MAT INSP.

OFFICE

125'

LUMBER STORAGE

PLATFORM

LOADING PLATFORM

ROAD   SIDING

FINISHED BOAT STORAGE

SERVICE STOCK ROOM

CAFETERIA

BOILER HOUSE

MACH. SHOP

…E DODGE BOAT AND PLANE CORP.

3589:A

Dodge's 1931 and 1932 21-foot, 6-inch split-cockpit runabout, with its long foredeck, modern twin Vee-windshields, and flared boot stripe, established attractive standards for designers to follow or try to exceed. *Robert Bruce Duncan*

Chapter Five

A New Beginning in Newport News

When the armistice was signed in November 1919, proclaiming the official end of World War I, a wave of optimism swept through America. The Great War was over and President Woodrow Wilson's new League of Nations was formed to ensure that such a devastating conflict would never again take place.

Industry in America thrived, employment was strong, and signs of prosperity reached an increasing number of American families. It was a time of wonderful new inventions that made life better and created more opportunities.

Surplus aircraft engines manufactured for military aircraft were converted into powerful marine engines for speedboats and express cruisers. Pleasure boating grew rapidly in popularity and became another new symbol of success.

Well-to-do sportsmen expressed greater interest in boating and especially enjoyed the excitement of fast powerboats. A growing number of craftsmen explored boat building as an opportunity to establish careers in a new and promising occupation. During the later part of the 1920s, boat building was touted as one of the next boom industries for investors, and unprecedented amounts of money were spent on boats throughout the decade.

The record-breaking sales at the 1929 National Motor Boat Show seemed to provide absolute proof that prosperity was firmly established and that boating was becoming the new leisure-time activity for a growing number of Americans. Financial groups searching for new growth industries considered family-operated boat builders such as Chris-Craft solid investment opportunities. With more orders than they could fill, boat builders across the nation entered major expansion programs to keep pace with the demand.

Expansion fever spread rapidly through nearly every significant boat-building firm as

they prepared for the sales boom that everyone anticipated. Boat builders looked forward to the 1930 National Motor Boat Show, convinced that new sales records would be achieved. Even when the stock market crashed on October 29, 1929, few people grasped its long-term repercussions for the economy. Only a handful of astute economists had any idea of the disaster that was happening.

Throwing Caution to the Wind

Most boat builders were conservative in nearly everything they did. They routinely built special boats with features that their clients requested to meet their individual wishes. Boat builders also didn't talk a great deal among one another, and as a result, they all had their individual, preferred techniques for constructing boats. Their work was often superb, but their methods were usually cumbersome when compared to industrial standards of manufacturing. Their clients, however, were almost always prosperous and didn't object to paying the additional cost for fine workmanship as evidence of their good taste.

For many boat builders, it took years of strong sales before they were finally ready and able to embrace the notion of expanding their facilities. Boat builders were craftsmen, and they traditionally occupied old buildings that were

The nearly completed Horace E. Dodge Boat and Plane factory in Newport News, Virginia, with 26 freight cars waiting at the railroad siding in the foreground.

often drafty, damp, crowded, dirty, and always prone to fire. In 1929 virtually the entire industry seemed to feel the surge of confidence necessary to expand or build new facilities.

When Horace Dodge's mother offered to build a new boat factory for him, he was so motivated that he renamed his company to reflect his intentions of building seaplanes along with an entire fleet of new boats. The Horace E. Dodge Boat and Plane Corporation was established in 1929 and began construction of a superbly engineered factory complex that would be the largest boat-building facility in the world upon completion in the spring of 1930.

Dodge's State-of-the-Art Facility

The site of the new Dodge factory in Newport News, Virginia, was based on a professionally conducted study. The land offered 2,100 feet of level shoreline on Hampton Roads directly across the bay from a U.S. Naval base and a U.S. Army terminal. Plus, the factory could be serviced by the Chesapeake & Ohio Railroad, which in turn

provided connections to all parts of the country and the world. The new factory plans included provisions for building two long rail spurs alongside each building to handle dozens of freight cars. In addition, the Newport News location was within close proximity to a vital seaport, offering a more economical way to export boats to foreign countries by eliminating the extra handling costs common to the former Detroit location.

Dodge insisted that his new factory would be the finest state-of-the-art boat-building facility that money could buy. Designed to support his requirements for straight-line production with absolute efficiency, the facility would be capable of producing the highest volume of runabouts in the industry. Dodge secured Philip L. Small and Associates of Ohio, considered one of the best industrial firms in the country, to design the new complex. Small's talented and most experienced designer, Beckwith Kofoed, was assigned to oversee the massive contract and organized a special team to study, design, and supervise the construction. At their first meeting, Kofoed and

A 1930–1931 split-cockpit 21-foot, 6-inch runabout (foreground) enjoys an informal race with a 1932–1936 dual-cockpit-forward 19-foot, 6-inch model. *Classic Boating Magazine*

Dodge agreed that the increased demand for boats seemed to confirm the obsolescence of traditional methods of boat construction.

As Kofoed studied boat production, he realized that the adoption of straight-line assembly methods offered not only an exciting alternative but also a difficult challenge. Various types of lumber, virtually the sole material in the construction of boats at that time, required a great deal of study and experimentation to achieve the desired result. Kofoed's immediate concerns were the proper handling of expensive lumber to avoid waste, the equalizing of the time required for various operations to maintain uniform flow, and the provision of working conditions conducive to the temperament of skilled workers with various individual abilities.

Kofoed's study showed that the typical Dodge runabout needed four major construction operations. It was estimated that 20 percent of the time would be devoted to cutting and shaping hull materials; 48 percent to building the hull; 13 percent to painting, staining, and varnishing; and 19 percent to installing hardware and the engine. For the straight-line production concept to work properly and achieve maximum efficiency, it was essential that production moved at a steady pace throughout the workday. This requirement was complicated by the reality of seasonal considerations connected to boating in many of the country's prime markets.

Selected for its proximity to discriminating markets; ready power sources; available living arrangements for employees; favorable weather; and good rail, highway, and shipping facilities, the new factory was strategically sited to accommodate Dodge's immediate needs and future development expected in the boat industry. In addition, the easy access to the ocean provided superb testing for rough-water conditions and the impact of saltwater on mechanical equipment and finishes, while the nearby James River was perfectly suited for freshwater testing. The site also offered ample room for seaplanes and amphibious aircraft to safely land and take off.

Dodge's selection of Philip L. Small and Associates to design the Newport News factory was a prudent decision. Including the subcontract with Racine Manufacturing, this was Dodge's third boat factory in six years, and he wanted nothing left to chance. Yet, once again, he returned to his home in England, leaving much of the responsibility to others.

With six years of experience refining Dodge's method for building boats, Horace's staff made sure that the architects thoroughly understood each step, department, and subassembly. Efficiency and economy were important aspects of Dodge's dream of providing boats for the average family, and even though Horace's mother was especially generous to the project, he couldn't help but feel with some certainty that he might

This early-1930 25-foot runabout, which was available through 1934, preceded a redesigned version introduced in 1931 and known as the 25-foot, 6-inch Special with a larger engine and greater speed.

not be given another chance if this effort failed. Philip Small's architects carefully studied each phase of production in the Detroit factory in order to fully understand the intricacies of building a typical Dodge boat.

In determining the required size of the factory, the designers were provided with the anticipated volume of boat sales for the next five to 10 years and then determined the production volume capability required for meeting this prediction. Experience predicted that each production line could make four or five 16-foot to 20-foot boats per day. Eight lines, then, could produce the volume necessary to meet the estimated demand. These lines would require service areas to provide a steady flow of hardware, upholstery, engines, and lumber to keep the lines moving efficiently without delays or interruption.

With the strong possibility that Dodge would begin building metal boats within the next three years, increased factory headroom also became a significant consideration. Metal boats would require huge stamping machinery, large metal die presses, and bending equipment. Even in 1930, boat builders were concerned over the scarcity of quality boat lumber and considered metal a reasonable alternative to wood construction. The factory planners determined that the height clearance in the low sections of the factory should be no less than 13 feet from

the floor to the underside of the roof beams and trusses. The standard clearance for the majority of the plant would be 18 feet from the floor to clear the monorail system track.

To compensate for the seasonal nature of the industry that traditionally resulted in regular layoffs, it was also deemed necessary to provide facilities to store fully or partially completed boats during the slower season. This holding area would provide an ample supply of boats during the rush season so that employment levels could remain somewhat constant throughout the calendar year.

The huge storage area, with more than 27,000 square feet, had the capacity to absorb several weeks of boat production while waiting for the peak selling season. To facilitate the efficient movement of boats in and out of this storage area, the building was equipped with narrow gauge railroad tracks, a special electric locomotive, and flatcars. The storage area purposely had a dirt floor to provide the necessary moisture content around the boats and protect the inventory from excessive drying.

Ironically, the Dodges awarded the construction contract just three days before the stock market crash in October 1929, and groundbreaking took place a week later on November 1. Construction of the main factory building, which measured 126x700 feet, used 575 tons of steel and

Top: Dodge negotiated an attractive contract with Lycoming to use their engines exclusively in all Dodge standardized runabouts. Dodge kept a generous supply on hand at all times.

Above: The Newport News factory featured unusually high ceilings, supply balconies, and abundant natural lighting. Shown in the foreground is one of the large bandsaws used to resaw expensive African mahogany lumber to proper dimensions for planking.

contained over 210,000 square feet of usable floor space. Other structures on the complex included a 78x340-foot boat-storage building, a 40x85-foot heating plant, a 30x75-foot office building, a 35x120-foot lumber-storage structure, and a watchman's house that measured 18x25 feet.

Designed to Eliminate Waste

Raw stock arrived at the Newport News factory primarily by railroad cars and was unloaded onto the internal, overhead monorail system through the receiving clerk's office at the north end of the plant. From there the monorail system distributed the materials to any location within the factory.

Supplies also could be transported to any location in the factory via an external monorail system located alongside the building above the loading platform. A separate building at the north end of the factory, equipped for air drying and curing, could store one-third of a million board feet of rough lumber that was used for keels, engine stringers, and frames.

Another lumber storage building on the west side of the factory was reserved for the valuable mahogany hardwoods that had been cured prior to delivery.

Future expansion plans called for a mill to cut mahogany logs and cure hardwood on site. When marine engines were received, they were transported on the outside monorail system to the south end of the factory where they were inspected and then block-tested before being stored in a section of the boat storage facility.

Following the straight-line production system, the next step was the milling department where patterns and templates were used to prepare each component of the hull's frame following the practice developed at Racine Manufacturing in 1924. The milling department was a state-of-the-art woodworking shop with modern equipment to cut, shape, sand, drill, plane, and otherwise prepare wood for final assembly. Tools included table saws, planers, shapers, band resaws, four surface moulders, and power-fed straight-line ripsaws.

The supply balcony concept was used effectively in the Newport News factory to store upholstery materials, completed frame sets, and production supplies within access to specific production areas and thus keep the lines moving efficiently.

Right: The extensive upholstery shop in the Newport News factory was located on one of the intermediate-level balconies efficiently situated above the production lines.

Below: This view shows the beginning of the 727-foot production line at Newport News. Here, the precut and pre-assembled frames for 16-foot utility models were attached to keels. The journey continued through a series of specialty assembly stations and finally to the end of the line and water-testing.

Everything was arranged in a careful pattern to eliminate any wasted motion and to promote efficiency. The finished parts from the mill were stored in overhead balconies until they were transported to a production line as determined by the material distribution schedule. All parts from the mill were thoroughly prepared before delivery to the assembly line. A large balcony above the mill was devoted to the upholstering shop where seat cushions and seatbacks were prepared according to the boat production schedule. The finished upholstered items were transferred directly to the installation department.

The assembly schedule required a specific number of finished pieces to be drawn from stock each night and delivered to the various stations via the monorail. The parts were placed in specially designed racks in the proper order in which they were to be assembled. The distribution of materials also included all the fittings, screws, and bolts required for the assembly procedures. A vital component of the system was the equalization of the labor time necessary to maintain an uninterrupted flow along the line.

The entire factory was designed to provide uniform distribution of light and ventilation. Three-quarters of the sidewalls were glass windows that provided excellent natural lighting. Banks of ventilators fed fresh air into each area while an exhaust system removed sawdust and shavings from each machine through metal ducts to the central heating system, where they were used to fuel the steam boilers and hot-water supply.

Abundant lockers and lavatories were provided in convenient locations within each department throughout the factory. In some departments there were shower stalls and rooms for employees to make necessary clothing changes if the nature of their work required it.

A section of the lumber-storage wing housed an attractive cafeteria where workers could relax briefly with their coworkers for a warm hearty meal or a snack. Food was prepared and sold at moderate prices or workers could bring their own meal. The amenities that Horace Jr. provided echoed the thoughtful way in which the Dodge brothers had treated their employees in Detroit and in 1930 were very advanced considerations.

Moving Down the Assembly Line

At the first stage in the straight-line assembly was the construction department where the keels were laid in the strongback and the frames were assembled and set into place. The planking also

The 1930 21-foot, 6-inch split-cockpit became one of Dodge's most distinguished runabouts, with a long foredeck, attractive twin folding windshields, and advanced styling years ahead of the field.

was attached here and the lifting eyes were installed so the hull could be transported on the monorail to the next station. After the hulls were planked, they proceeded into the sanding room where large portable electric disc sanders removed any surface irregularities. The area was enclosed with four-fold doors at each end of the room while the disc sanders generated vast quantities of dust.

The dust-laden air was exhausted continuously and the hulls were cleaned further with jets of compressed air and vacuums before they left the sanding room. The sanding operation took a great deal of strength and skill. Any lapse of concentration or careless mistake could create a serious blemish in an otherwise perfect hull. The work was hot, noisy, tiring, and dirty, and the men assigned to the duty spent their entire workday in a type of isolation from everyone else in the plant.

From the sanding department, the hull moved to a second construction station where the deck planking, combing, sealing boards, seat frames, and transoms were installed. After this stage, the hull was essentially complete; the only parts left off the hull were those that might interfere with the smooth installation of the engine. However, these parts were already carefully fitted to the appropriate hull, stamped with the proper hull number, and sanded, accompanying the hull to the painting and finishing department, which

was entirely closed off at each end with sets of large folding doors.

It was vital that all dust was eliminated from the paint room and that the precise temperature and humidity for optimum finishing was maintained. A minimum of air circulation also was required to avoid the transfer of any dust to a freshly applied finish. Filtered air, heated to the correct temperature, was introduced continuously through overhead supply ducts while fumes were removed through grilles that were located in the floor and connected to a duct system. Exhaust fans removed the foul air a safe distance away from the building. Storage rooms for paints, stains, sealers, varnishes, and solvents were located in special fireproof rooms sheathed in metal and furnished with fireproof shelving.

When the painting was completed, the transfer bay, which was partially in the paint department and partially in the installation department, moved each boat either onto another assembly line or to the installation department. From there, the boat was either moved to the storage facility, transferred to the special construction department where features such as sedan enclosures were added, or moved directly to the loading platform.

The installation department was where finishing details were applied, including metal

Right: After reaching the end of one of seven Newport News production lines, completed runabouts were required to be water-tested before they could be approved for shipment to any of one hundred franchised Dodge boat dealers throughout North America.

Below: A 21-foot, 6-inch 1930 runabout is lifted by crane and launched for its test run as required of the final inspection in Dodge's standard procedure.

fittings, hardware, upholstery, windshields, gas tanks, shafts, propellers, electrical wiring, the engine, and engine hatches. This department included storage areas for metal parts, dash instrument panels, and storage batteries, and had several machines for metalworking. The plant superintendent's office was located on the balcony directly over the installation department with an unobstructed view of the plant's interior on one side and the launching platform on the other side.

After the boats were completed and inspected, they were ready for their required water test. The large, full-height doors at the south, or waterfront, end of the factory were opened and the boats lifted by a huge gantry crane that traveled on steel tracks. These tracks ran the full width of the plant and lined up with the assembly line monorails for easy transfer to the crane. The gantry crane was operated electrically from a cab and traveled at a rate of 150 feet per minute with safety devices of every description, including automatic stops at the loading and unloading points.

The crane lifted the boat from the platform and carried it to position with a cantilevered arm over the wet slip. The boat was then lowered into the water where the gas tank was filled with enough fuel for its test run. A checklist featured several predetermined activities and space for assessments detailing any necessary adjustments. After the water test was completed, the boat was lifted again by the gantry crane and returned to the factory.

In the shipping department the boat was cleaned and inspected before it was packed, cradled, and prepared for shipment. From there the boat was transferred via the monorail system to a railroad boxcar or another delivery vehicle, or was loaded on a barge to be delivered to a steamer for overseas shipment to any location in the world.

The Newport News factory was a masterpiece of superb planning. Kofoed and his team of engineers created the entire complex around Dodge's production concepts and the practical wisdom and experience of William Horn, a well-known and popular figure in the boating

After successfully going through the final inspection, 16-foot utilities are loaded into Chesapeake & Ohio Railroad freight cars for distribution to Dodge dealers.

world who had been with Dodge since the Atwater Street factory opened in 1924. The team studied every phase of the Dodge system in detail and planned for both immediate needs and future growth.

H.E.'s Lieutenants

Horace's mother insisted that her personal financial consultant and attorney, J. Gilmore Fletcher, was named first vice president and managing director of the new venture. Although Horace was president, Fletcher was actually the person responsible for the daily business operations. Fletcher communicated with Horace frequently, but Dodge had other interests and made no plans to establish residence in Newport News, Virginia.

The new $2 million factory opened on March 13, 1930, with complete coverage by *The Newport News Daily Press*. The headlines quoted Dodge's forecast of producing 4,000 boats in the factory's first year and reported, "Opening of the

The attractive interior of Dodge's new Manhattan showroom and national sales office opened in 1929 with the $15,000 Sterling Silver Dodge Memorial Trophy on display alongside models of the Dodge family yachts *Delphine* and *Nokomis II.*

new plant was celebrated with all of the civic organizations of Newport News organizing a huge banquet for the Dodge officials."

At the opening, Fletcher met with eager reporters who expressed concern about the impact that the depressed economy might have on Dodge boat sales. Fletcher responded by telling a *New York Sun* reporter:

There has been no general depression in the motor boat industry. With us 1930 has been a good year in spite of the inevitable delays and complications attendant upon the creation of the world's largest motor boat factory and embarkation upon a hitherto undreamed-of motor boat production schedule. We expect that the National Motor Boat Show to be, as it was last year, the bright spot in American industry at the turn of the new year. It will be an index to the bettered conditions for the coming twelve months. With one spectacular addition to our line of boats and improvements in our present models, we

intend to go after business just as if there had been no let down in commerce whatever. This decision was reached after careful and thorough discussions with our 200 distributors throughout the world. The boat business is not depressed. It is facing a prosperity such as it has never enjoyed before. All our resources are being employed to meet it.

Fletcher's optimistic statements proved to be more positive posturing than substantial.

The key player in getting production under way and keeping Horace's boat business in order was William Horn, an experienced and very successful race-boat driver of exceptional boat-building skills who was well respected by the entire Newport News workforce. In letters to Horn's daughter, his racing mechanic Charlie Grafflin reported that Horn and his crew, like the workers at Atwater Street, always referred to Dodge as H.E., again a reference to Horace Elgin. Horace, who was never fond of his given name, didn't seem to object, as the Atwater Street crew

had feared he would, and even appeared to enjoy its informality, which made him feel closer to key personnel at the factory.

Responsible for developing and styling each of the new Dodge runabouts was the young and talented Walter Leveau, who was appointed chief designer at Newport News. Whoever was hired to follow the legendary George Crouch as Dodge's new designer faced a significant challenge. However, Leveau's design skill became immediately apparent when his 1930 fleet of Dodge runabouts debuted to rave reviews at the National Motor Boat Show. His fresh, crisp designs set a standard that other major builders would scramble to follow.

The new factory superintendent in charge of production was Earl R. Hatten, a graduate of Rensselaer Polytechnic Institute and Massachusetts Institute of Technology. Prior to coming to

Dodge, Hatten's wide range of experience included stints commanding six navy submarine chasers, engineering for Wolverine Oil Company, and managing the Hickman Sea Sled Company plant, where his accomplishments received national attention. Plus, he was put in charge of production at the old factory in Detroit before inaugurating production in Newport News.

At the same time, the company moved from its sales offices from East 52nd Street in Manhattan to a new 4,000-square-foot national sales headquarters at 21 West 46th Street. The larger location permitted the display of all Dodge models and several Lycoming engines. Kenneth N. Smith, Dodge's national director of sales and marketing, then announced that the company had appointed more than 100 franchised dealers and distributors worldwide since January 1, 1930.

The start of the popular 50-mile Dodge-Sixteen Sweepstakes Race with 30 standardized 16-foot Dodge runabouts at the 1931 Harmsworth Trophy Regatta. The concept of one-design racing with inexpensive stock boats provided valuable publicity for Dodge.

With the introduction of the 21-foot, 6-inch split-cockpit runabout in 1930, Dodge designer Walter Leveau established a new benchmark for design excellence among contemporary runabout builders. *Robert Bruce Duncan*

Before joining Dodge, Smith was president of the Gould Storage Battery Company and during World War I served in Washington as executive secretary to the national director of aircraft production. Smith's assistant was L. S. Devos, who left a similar position with Chris-Craft to join Dodge. Other key members of the new Dodge sales staff included F. F. Schryver, who brought 15 years of commercial banking experience to the company's booming New York district; Earl Lathrop, who took over the New England territory; and George Reiss, formerly of the Plymouth Motor Car Company and a New York–area distributor for Hupmobile automobiles. Corporate directors were Anna Dodge Dillman and Hugh Dillman. By January 1930 Dodge had plenty of talent in place to handle the output of the new production center in Newport News.

With its new corporate name, management positions filled, a complement of 700 workers covering three shifts, and a fleet of new models, the Horace E. Dodge Boat and Plane Corporation also had an absentee owner residing in Michigan and an absentee president 1,000 miles away—when he wasn't residing in Europe. At any other time this might have been a workable arrangement. This, however, was 1930 and the national economy was in a downward spiral that would hit rock bottom within two years. It was a time that would challenge even the most astute and experienced corporate executives just to

keep their factories operating. Yet, totally insulated from the realities of the economic impact of the times, Dodge was again off to Europe. The *New York Post* reported, "Mr. Dodge is also in charge of the department of foreign research and will spend most of his time visiting European boat building and aircraft factories, studying their methods and establishing Dodge dealerships throughout Europe."

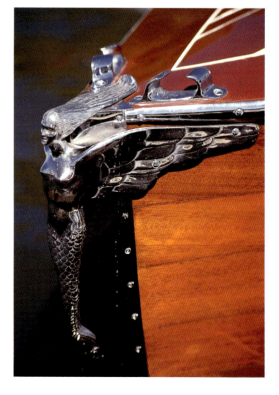

Right: Dodge's Sea Nymph, designed by the celebrated artist and sculptor Russell C. Crook, graced the bow of every Dodge runabout built after 1930. *Classic Boating Magazine*

More Attention Grabbing

To commemorate his new factory and his new fleet of trendy runabouts, Dodge once again upstaged his competition with an unusual new feature. In a special press release it was announced that the bow of every new Dodge would be graced with a distinctive figurehead. The artistic nickel silver adornment was the graceful figure of a winged sea nymph located on the uppermost section of the each boat's brightly polished cutwater. This distinctive attention-grabber was clearly a throwback to Dodge's automotive legacy and a vivid reminder of his connection to the success and reliability of the Dodge automobile.

The attractive figurehead was commissioned to Russell G. Crook, one of America's best-known sculptors, and presented the new Dodge models with a distinctive look, unlike any other runabout of the time. Dodge fully anticipated that other boat builders would replicate his idea and told reporters, "I expect that our new figurehead will start a fashion trend among American craft. During the next couple of years figureheads on runabouts and cruisers will be as varied and attractive as the radiator cap ornaments on our automobiles." There was no question that the flying sea nymph provided Dodge boats with a unique appearance. However, Dodge's optimistic forecast of a popular new trend among boat builders never materialized.

The complete 1930 fleet of Dodge boats consisted of four standard runabout models

The most popular model of all Dodge standardized production boats was the 16-foot runabout, which remained in production for five years without any significant changes.

Appearing only as an illustration, the 1930 Dodge 45-foot Express Cruiser remains shrouded in mystery. In the absence of actual photographs, it is presumed it was never actually constructed.

A Dodge runabout photographed in the setting sun gives pause to reflect on the remarkable innovations produced by Horace Dodge Jr.'s creative and highly productive organization. *Robert Bruce Duncan*

ranging from 16 to 28 feet. Each 1930 model featured an entirely new, Leveau-designed hull, creating another new generation of Dodge runabouts. There was also reference in the 1930 Dodge literature to a 45-foot, double-cabin Express Cruiser powered by twin V-12 Lycoming engines. There is, however, no record that this boat was ever produced, and the only illustration found in all the Dodge records was an artist's rendering.

Breaking from the Past

The 1930 Leveau models presented very smart, modern styling with attractive Vee-windshields raked back at a sharp angle and offering the advantage of folding flush to the deck to increase the feeling of speed. The new stem design, in contrast to the very rounded stem previously

used on models designed by Crouch, resembled the more formal look used by Gar Wood. The contrived model name Watercar no longer seemed appropriate and was quietly abandoned starting with the 1930 models, never to be used again. Stylish oval step pads replaced Dodge's original rectangular style; surrounded by bright nickel silver oval rings, the white rubber step pads featured the name "Dodge" in raised letters above a diamond pattern. The most significant design element of the new Dodge runabouts, however, was the a totally modern flush-deck styling. Even Chris-Craft, often recognized for setting styling trends, was still building four somewhat dated raised-deck runabout models in 1930. The 1930 Dodges were all new, without so much as a design cue taken from previous models. The new boats employed double-

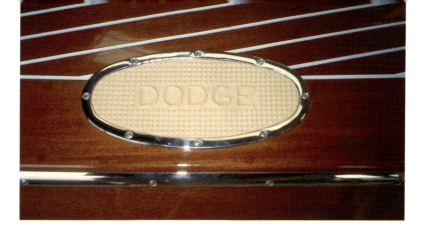

planked bottom construction using a layer of marine canvas sandwiched between the two mahogany skins. The canvas was impregnated with marine canvas cement to provide a strong bottom that was resistant to the problems of leaky seams. All the planking on the decks, sides, bottoms, transoms, and bulkheads was selected African mahogany, and the inner seams between each plank were reinforced with a longitudinal

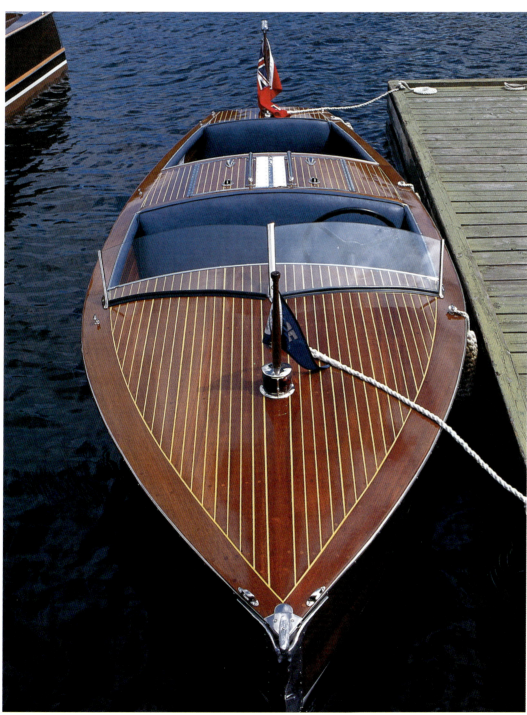

Above: From 1930 on, Dodge step pads were restyled in white rubber with a diamond texture and "Dodge" in raised letters, officially closing the "Watercar" era.

Left: The 16-foot Dodge dual-cockpit runabout introduced in 1930 was their most popular model and kept the production lines moving throughout the Great Depression. *Robert Bruce Duncan*

The new Dodge brain trust responsible for the operation of Newport News met aboard the yacht *Delphine* in early 1929. From left to right: Kenneth M. Smith, director of sales; R. S. Simpers of advertising; J. Gillmore Fletcher, managing director and vice president; Horace E. Dodge Jr., president; Earl R. Hatten, factory superintendent; and William Horn, production manager and secretary-treasurer.

batten. All fastenings were of bronze and brass, and struts and rudders of manganese bronze were used with shafts of Monel metal. Solid nickel silver was the choice for all deck fittings, and a pleasant shade of green antifouling paint was standard for the bottoms of all models.

In another effort to set Dodge apart from the competition, the company announced plans to use Lycoming engines exclusively in all new models. Lycoming was a branch of the Auburn Automobile Company, makers of the luxurious Auburn, Cord, and 265-horsepower Duesenberg automobiles. With Horace planning to make seaplanes, Lycoming also could have provided him with aircraft engines. At the time, Lycoming was making motors for the Stinson Aircraft Company, another subsidiary of Auburn. Initially, Dodge reportedly ordered 3,000 marine engines and soon after requested an additional 1,200 engines. The entire order for 4,200 engines was planned for delivery in 1930.

Dodge's "Loss Leader"

Dodge's low-price entry for 1930 was a 16-foot split-cockpit runabout with one cockpit forward of the engine compartment and another aft of the engine. It was an attractive, sporty craft intended to attract first-time buyers and was very suitable for the small lakes where summer cottages were springing up throughout the Northeast and Midwest. An enlarged version of the split-cockpit seating arrangement with an abundance of deluxe features was the 21-foot runabout, equipped with attractive folding "Vee-windshields" fore and aft. This runabout has become a favorite among classic-boat enthusiasts with its unique styling, solid performance, and ease of trailing to summer boat shows. Dodge's 25-foot and 28-foot runabouts for 1930 also were both triple-cockpit models equipped with dual folding Vee-windshields. The Dodge 1930 catalog was printed with 22 color illustrations prominently featuring the prices for each model and was published in its entirety in the 1930 show

issues of the major boating magazines. It was a marvelous marketing achievement for such a young company.

Building the 16-foot runabout was a new experience for Dodge, but the company deemed it necessary to maintain their promise of building affordable boats and to expand their market share. The Dodge team believed that if they could encourage first-time buyers to begin with a Dodge boat, then they could keep them moving up within the Dodge fleet. To reaffirm that goal, the 16-foot, five-passenger runabout was offered at $945, strategically under $1,000, and came with the standard 40-horsepower Lycoming engine. However, its price provided very little profit margin. Even though it was their price leader, Dodge never intended it to become their dominant-selling boat. Dodge's initial marketing concept anticipated that their three larger runabouts would become their bestselling models. As the national economy continued to slide, however, Dodge dealers

Top: The 25-foot 1930 Model 4 with the 165-horsepower Lycoming straight-eight engine offered a top speed of 38 miles per hour and demonstrated Dodge's flair for progressive styling. *Harold Orchard*

Above: The instrument panel on Dodge's deluxe runabouts was exceptionally attractive, with five easy-to-read instrument gauges decorated with twin Sea Nymphs. *Classic Boating Magazine*

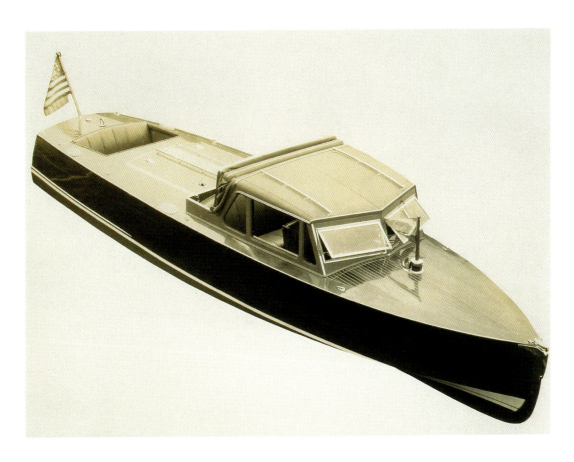

considered it less risky to stock the inexpensive 16-foot models than the larger models. Unfortunately, the 16-footer began to dominate Dodge's production lines during the Depression years, ending up as Dodge's highest-volume model by a large margin.

When Dodge was forced to lower prices as the Depression dragged on, the cost of building each 16-footer soon exceeded the net wholesale cost that their dealers paid the manufacturer. Each time a shipment of 16-footers left the factory, Dodge lost money. The intended role for this little runabout before the depressed economy prevailed was to stimulate interest in the more profitable models by enticing prospects into dealer's showrooms with a Dodge

This attractive view of the 1930 Dodge 25-foot runabout shows its full deck layout and roomy aft cockpit with a windshield to protect passengers from wind and spray. It's powered by a Lycoming straight eight, providing speeds up to 38 miles per hour. *Classic Boating Magazine*

boat for less than $1,000. The plan seemed logical, but dealers were delighted to move the small runabouts whenever they were able. The larger, more profitable models were simply not as well suited for the majority of buyers in the depressed economy.

The 21-foot runabout with its twin folding windshields and 35-mile-per-hour speed was

Left: At full throttle, the Lycoming 115- to 125-horsepower Model UC straight eight-cylinder 322ci displacement engine in the 21-foot, 6-inch Dodge runabout turns 3,000 to 3,200 rpms.

Below: The popular 16-foot runabouts in the final stages of production enter the engine-installation department prior to moving outside for the water test and final inspection checklist.

With Newport News' seven production lines operating at full capacity, 40 new boats were completed and inspected each day.

wonderfully attractive and very sporty. The split-cockpit arrangement was unique for a boat of its length. However, priced at $2,100, the Dodge 21-footer had to compete with two popular Chris-Craft models of similar length that offered three cockpits rather than just two: the 20-foot triple cockpit for $1,895 and the 22-foot triple cockpit at $2,195. Despite Dodge's styling advantage, Chris-Craft's three cockpits for a similar price were enough to lure away buyers. The standard engine for the 21-foot model, which actually measured 21 feet, 6 inches, was the straight eight-cylinder Lycoming rated at 115 horsepower.

Dodge's attractive 25-foot triple-cockpit runabout was offered with a deluxe Kroh sedan top by mid-1930. The open version (Model 3), priced at $2,500, was equipped with twin folding windshields, and standard power was a 125-horsepower Lycoming straight eight producing speeds up to 32 miles per hour. The Model 4 offered the optional 165-horsepower Lycoming straight eight that attained speeds to 38 miles per hour for $3,200. The sedan version of the 25-footer was designated as the Model 10 and offered at $3,900. In 1930 Gar Wood did not have a runabout in this length, and Chris Craft's

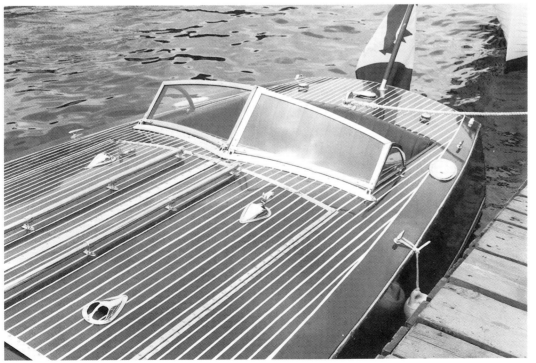

Above: In 1930, racer Frank Wigglesworth of Boston, Massachusetts, won the 50-mile, $6,000 Dodge-Sixteen Sweepstakes in Detroit, promoting the significance of Horace Dodge's standardized boats.

Left: With their successful 1930 runabouts, Dodge designers set new standards with smart styling that included practical folding Vee-windshields fore and aft on their deluxe models.

93

Right: Lycoming's 300-horsepower V-12 displaced 1,010ci and provided excellent speed and power for the bigger Dodge runabouts. It was also praised as a fine value during the Depression. *Classic Boating Magazine*

Below: Dealers were surprised by the 25-foot, 6-inch Dodge runabout, with its gleaming white hull, was introduced in 1931 as a wider, stronger version of the original 1930 25-foot runabout, capable of handling the Lycoming's 325-horsepower V-12 and speeds to 48 miles per hour.

26-footer was $700 more with similar power and a dated image.

In 1930 a few owners reported that the 25-foot runabouts were rather "tender" and a bit unsettling when running in rough seas. There might have been some merit to these early complaints, because Dodge later incorporated structural changes to the model to stiffen the bottom. In addition, Dodge introduced an entirely new 25-foot, 6-inch model in 1931 with improved lines and increased the beam by 5 inches. However, they continued to offer both models in 1931 and again in 1933 before the 25-footer was permanently discontinued.

The flagship of Dodge's runabout fleet for 1930 was the beautifully designed and impressively performing 28-footer with a 7-foot, 5-inch beam. The contemporary Chris-Craft and Gar Wood models at this length were excellent boats, but not nearly as attractive as the Dodge, which featured a rakish Vee-windshield for both the forward and the aft cockpits long before either of its two rivals. The standard engine for the Model 5 was the 165-horse-power Lycoming straight eight producing speeds of 32 miles per hour for $3,700. The Model 6 outfitted the 28-footer with a 300-horsepower Lycoming V-12. This engine, which was available in limited supply, provided thrilling speeds in the range of 45 miles per hour. To go this fast, buyers had to shell out $4,500. The 28-foot runabout also was offered as the Model 11 with a sedan or limousine top and the V-12 engine for an additional $800. The Dodge prices were significantly less than those of similar models offered by Gar Wood.

The Dodge sedan cabins were manufactured in Toledo, Ohio, by the C. Z. Kroh Company and shipped to Newport News for installation on standard runabout hulls by Dodge employees. Kroh also manufactured similar cabin enclosures for Chris-Craft, Gar Wood, and other runabout builders. It was a costly option but very popular, offering the advantages of shade on a hot day and shelter on cool or rainy days. Owners enjoyed a longer boating season with these automotive-style enclosures.

The Dodge sedan cabin was technically the landau-style top, with the fabric aft section folding up and forward to meet the roofline. This style provided a complete opening over the cabin's aft bench seat, providing a more open feeling when the weather was pleasant and allowing easier access in or out of the enclosure. The standard limousine configuration had a sliding hatch located over the center section of the cabin's aft bench seat. While this provided a snug enclosure, Dodge felt that it was a bit too confining and preferred to offer the landau style.

The flagship of the new 1930 Dodge fleet was the 28-foot, 7-inch triple-cockpit. With its V-12 Lycoming engine, it provided speeds up to 46 miles per hour and remained in production through 1935.

The center-mounted nautical wheel in the 1935 Model 304 16-foot utility identified as the "Fishing Boat" used a pulley system to help keep the cost under $500. *Gary Michael*

Chapter Six

The Struggle for Survival

As more articles appeared in boating journals detailing Dodge's innovative concepts, the company began to attract the attention of Horace's favorite rival, Gar Wood. Like many other successful boat builders, Gar Wood also was convinced by the unparalleled success of the 1929 National Motor Boat Show that it was time to expand production and build a new factory. Wood decided to locate his new factory site in Marysville, a growing community eager to attract new industry that was a few miles upriver from his existing plant in Algonac, just north of Detroit.

The Marysville site allowed Wood to employ the same well-trained personnel and continue to use the same suppliers with whom they were familiar. Wood wisely negotiated an extremely favorable long-term property tax moratorium along with scores of other incentives. Similar to Dodge, the new, extremely efficient Gar Wood factory utilized straight-line production, but it was considerably smaller than the immense new Dodge plant.

Not to be outdone by Dodge's claim of building "the world's largest boat factory," Wood simply referred to his new facility as "the world's finest boat factory." The new Gar Wood fleet for 1930 consisted of three runabout models of 22, 28, and 33 feet, plus limousine options for the 28- and 33-footers. The rivalry among Dodge and Gar Wood and Chris-Craft started to heat up as their styling and model offerings became remarkably similar and the number of potential buyers did not increase as rapidly as previously anticipated.

Dodge's assembly concept for standardized models provided much of the efficiency that he predicted. There was no question that his theory could be applied successfully to the production of boats. However, the cost benefits anticipated from volume production required equally vigorous, high-volume marketing, merchandising, and sales efforts in order for the production to be consumed.

To the Depths of Depression

As the ripple effect from the Wall Street meltdown on Black Monday in 1929 began to erode consumer confidence, boat sales began to decline. The slump was hardly noticeable at first, but by the time the all-new boat factories were nearing completion, it was painfully evident that sales projections for 1930 had slipped perilously. Cautious but not discouraged, the boating industry predicted that sales for 1931 would show solid gains similar to 1929.

Dealers attending the 1931 National Motor Boat Show, however, remained conservative and their orders modest. In 1930 national pleasure boat sales were off by 15 percent. In 1931 boat sales dropped by an additional 60 percent—the industry was in serious trouble. Employee layoffs were rampant and many builders of small boats and marine dealerships were forced

to close. Even the well-financed Horace E. Dodge Boat and Plane Corporation had to reduce production; its new, unsold boats were simply moving directly from the factory into the storage building that was already filled to capacity. Dodge's only active production line was devoted to runabout models, and even they seemed to be too extravagant for the depressed American economy.

It was time for boat builders to step back, review their costs, and determine if lower prices might be the answer to attracting the more cautious buyers. Before the middle of 1931, Walter Leveau and his design team prepared plans for the new model that they believed would fill the void in their lineup. The new boat, called the All-Purpose 19-footer, was planked and decked with the more economical Philippine "hardwood" rather than expensive African mahogany and was finished with white paint instead of the more costly stain and varnish finish. The new boat was given a short forward deck and the rest was completely open with its 45-horsepower engine under a hardwood box. The caption over the boat at the 1932 National Motor Boat Show shouted, "This is the boat the world has waited for at a price the world can pay!"

The First Utility Model Is Born

The All-Purpose, identified as Model 202, was the very first production utility model from any major builder. The *New York Sun* ran a feature story about the new boat, describing its uniqueness by stating, "Stability is obtained through its unusually broad beam and is heightened by its design with a heavy keel, carried aft to protect the propeller against drift wood and beaching or grounding." The 19-footer was offered at the low price of $695.

Born out of the Depression, this important craft would open the door to an entirely new concept for utilitarian sport boats that, in time, would replace the slick runabouts in overall popularity, styling, and performance. The description of the early Dodge utility appearing in company brochures and advertisements expressed its versatility:

The newest Dodge creation is a boat designed especially for the entire family. Safe, comfortable and roomy, yet trim, fast and beautiful, it is as well suited for long, lazy

Dodge's popular Model 2 built from 1932 to 1934 could accommodate several passengers with its large open cockpit. It was capable of 18 miles per hour with its basic 45-horsepower four-cylinder Lycoming engine.

fishing trips and all day outings, as it is for short, quick jaunts and thrilling dashes over sun-kissed waves. It provides ample room for eight or more people with plenty of space left over for fishing tackle, hunting outfits, duffel bags, food hampers or any other luggage you may want to carry. Camp chairs may be set up in the rear of the cockpit to provide additional seating capacity or to allow you to fish in comfort.

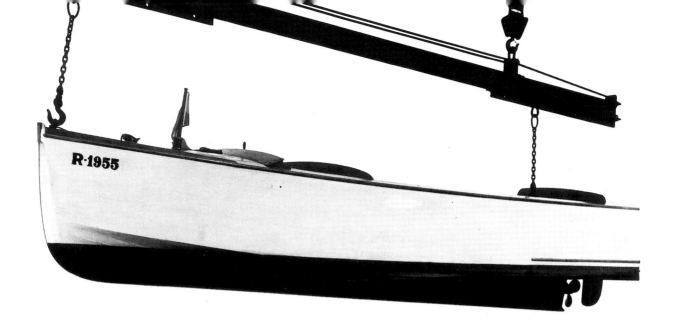

For an additional $100, a buyer could purchase the All-Purpose Model 203 finished with stain and varnish. Soon, lumber suppliers conveniently replaced the term *Philippine hardwood* with *Philippine mahogany*, and a more acceptable-sounding species emerged exclusively for the boat industry.

As with the 16-foot runabout in 1930, the utility models provided so little profit margin that the shipping cradle usually included with all boats was not included in the advertised price. However, the all-purpose craft was popular with Dodge dealers and sold well enough to encourage more developments of the style for 1933. The handsome 21-foot runabout was dropped from production, and in its place Dodge introduced a 19-foot, 5-inch runabout with a double cockpit forward and a single cockpit aft of the engine. It was an interesting little boat that somehow managed to accommo-

Seven passengers sitting along the starboard gunwale demonstrate the inherent stability of the Model 2, whose hull was nearly as wide at the waterline as it was at the sheer.

date three cockpits in its relatively short length. The boat's real significance, however, was that it gave Dodge dealers a triple-cockpit runabout that they could sell for only $1,385.

Another new runabout for 1932 was a 23-foot, 5-inch triple-cockpit model with dual windshields and speeds up to 32 miles per hour. It was offered with a Lycoming straight eight producing speeds up to 37 miles per hour. The new model was priced at $1,995 with a six-cylinder 90-horsepower engine and at $2,295 with the 125-horsepower straight eight.

The 25-foot, 6-inch runabout introduced in 1931 with the powerful V-12 engine as standard was made available with a more modest straight eight engine at $3,195.

Prices for the 28-foot runabout models remained the same. Perhaps it was understood that the small numbers of customers able to afford larger runabouts would not be influenced by reduced prices as an added incentive to acquire a boat of this stature. Dodge offered the custom Kroh enclosed sedan options on their 25- and 28-foot runabouts for an additional $800.

Taking the Gold Cup to Detroit

The bright news for 1932 occurred when *Delphine IV*, Horace Dodge's backup race boat at the Gold Cup Regatta with Bill Horn driving, won the event. As the owner of the boat, Horace was awarded the trophy and officially declared the winner of the prestigious regatta, a victory

Above: In 1932 Dodge introduced the shortest standardized triple-cockpit runabout on the market with its 19-foot, 5-inch Model 204 priced at just $1,385. With speeds up to 34 miles per hour, the boat was an attempt to stimulate more interest in stylish runabouts.

Left: The owners of two stylish Dodge runabouts take part in a casual race. A 1932–1936 dual-cockpit-forward 19-foot, 6-inch runabout pulls ahead of the 1930–1931 model split-cockpit 21-foot, 6-inch Dodge in the foreground. *Classic Boating Magazine*

Bill Horn, the talented race-boat driver and winner of the 1932 Gold Cup Regatta with *Delphine IV*, is remembered as Horace Jr.'s key employee, managing production in Detroit and Newport News and servicing race boats.

he cherished even though it was due to Horn's efforts. Horace had driven his newer boat, *Delphine V,* and was forced to drop out during the first heat with mechanical trouble.

In the years immediately preceding the 1932 Gold Cup, Horace had begun to slip into disfavor among Detroit racing enthusiasts. He was so frustrated with his disappointing racing performances that he often took out his emotions on local racers and race committees. After he moved his Detroit-based boat operations to Virginia, he spent a great deal of his personal time in England. When Bill Horn won the 1932 Gold Cup for Dodge, *Power Boat* magazine writer Ben Price explained:

For years, on and off, Horace, the Peck's bad boy of Detroit boating circles, had made

sallies after the Gold Cup. He had shown courage and no little perseverance, admirable qualities, but he had never gotten anywhere. And that is always tough on the home folks who began to expect that he had been fooling around. When he got away from the more orthodox paths of boat and building construction, they were sure of it. It was his time, his money and his neck, but you know how some folks can be. When he came out last year with Miss Syndicate III, *powered by an engine with so many cylinders that nobody ever bothered to count them, there was an agonized groan heard throughout the racing world. The boat was a horse, and as one biting critic declared might have done well on a good fast dirt track, provided she discarded her engine. She was large and unwieldy on the turns.*

A 1933 view of Dodge's straight-line production of 16-foot utility models shows four-cylinder Lycoming engines on the left, awaiting installation as the boats neared the end of the 727-foot line.

Then, when word got out that Dodge was having a new boat built for this year's race from plans by a foreign designer, there was another wave of agitation along the banks of the old Detroit River. The boys figured that he was high-hatting them, too.

The new design carried the suggestion of Kaye Don's boats, and in Detroit that was treason. Then, when it became known that the new boat was to be powered by the engine from last year's unfortunate entry (he's a

persistent devil), there was a howl that shook the sea fisheries. But now, all is forgiven. Horace may come home and with him is the Gold Cup last seen around Detroit almost a decade ago.

Dodge may continue to experiment, and likely he will. It would seem that he has plenty of material on hand to work with. His latest two boats have not rung the bell, but undoubtedly offer further possibilities. Dodge's flair for experimentation may have

Priced at $525, the 16-foot Model 301 lapstrake cedar utility of 1933 was an affordable option in a depressed economy. With its 40-horsepower four-cylinder engine, it could reach 25 miles per hour.

contributed more to the winning of this year's cup than indicated on the surface.

As it turned out, *Delphine V* was designed by Britain's Fred Cooper specifically to compete in the 1932 Gold Cup Regatta and was built in Newport News. With Horace taking the wheel of the new boat, he asked Bill Horn to drive the seven-year-old Gold Cup veteran *Delphine IV* in the race as backup. Since Dodge owned both boats, entered them, and approved all of the changes, if either boat won, it was his victory, regardless of the pilot at the wheel.

The race ended quickly for *Delphine V*. In the third lap of the first heat, its oil pressure fell to dangerous levels and its rear-mounted Duesenberg engine seized up. Dodge said later that he also experienced great difficulty holding it on its points. Meanwhile, Bill Horn, in *Delphine IV*, drove an excellent race in the older George Crouch–designed boat that had been reshingled and given few improvements over the years. Horn twice beat the existing 30-mile heat record and established a new mark for the total 90-mile course at 57.8 miles per hour. It was a gratifying victory for Dodge, and he triumphantly brought the Gold Cup back to Detroit determined to defend it successfully from all challengers in 1933.

A Crushing Defeat

Back at the boat factory in Newport News, Dodge moved away from the All-Purpose model name in 1933 in favor of the term "utility" for its

For an additional $100, the 19-foot Utility was available with a small shelter cabin that never won awards for design, but became a practical option that helped Dodge reach a few more customers.

expanded line of new models. The new 16-foot model, with a 45-horsepower Lycoming engine and painted hull, was offered at the low price of $545. The popular 19-foot utility hull was offered as an open model for $695 and with a small cabin enclosure for $795. The cabin model also offered an optional six-cylinder 66-horsepower engine for an additional $400.

There was no question that the utility style was gaining interest and helping keep Dodge's production lines active and moving during the worst period of the Depression. However, its stark appearance still provided a sharp contrast to the superb style of Dodge's very attractive runabouts. At the same time, Dodge runabout prices were being reduced once more in an effort to encourage more sales activity. The 16-foot runabout dipped from a high of $1,095 in 1931 to $795 in 1933. Without any explanation the attractive 23-foot, 5-inch runabout introduced in 1932 was dropped from its lineup after just one season. It was equally surprising to see the previously discontinued 25-foot runabout reappear in the 1934 Dodge specifications and illustrated in its 1934 catalog.

Horace, however, was nearly consumed with plans to defend the Gold Cup Trophy successfully at the 1933 race in Detroit. He wanted to win with another Fred Cooper design and just as stubbornly insisted on using the same style 12-cylinder Duesenberg engine that failed in 1932. His new boat was the British-built *Delphine IX*, which bore a strong resemblance to the Harmsworth challenger *Miss England II*, also designed by Cooper.

At the start of the first heat, George Reis, in *El Lagarto*, jumped into the lead and was followed most of the way by Jack Rutherford in *Imp*; Bill Horn, driving *Delphine IV*; Horace's sister, Delphine Dodge Baker, in *Delphine VII*; *Delphine VI*, piloted by F. G. Ericson; and finally by Horace in *Delphine IX*.

Horace's sister had been racing for some time by 1933, joining other women who had been successful in the sport, including Marion Carstairs, who had challenged Gar Wood in the 1928 Harmsworth race.

The new *Delphine IX* showed signs of excellent performance, but once again the engine failed to provide the speed needed to stay with the leaders. In the second heat, Horace relinquished the wheel to Benny Hill to see if he could coax improved performance out of the big Duesenberg. *Delphine IX* actually caught the leader in the backstretch of lap two but was forced to drop out by the fourth lap when the oil pressure dropped into the red zone.

In the final heat, *Delphine IX* was forced out with a broken connecting rod and *El Lagarto* cruised home with the Gold Cup. Bill Horn in *Delphine IV* set a new record for 625ci class boats, averaging 60.3 miles per hour. Horace's insistence on sticking with a Duesenberg engine that couldn't stand up to the rigors of Gold Cup racing kept him out of contention once again.

Horace was crushed by the defeat. He used four superb boats, all named *Delphine*, to defend his hold on the Gold Cup in his home waters of the Detroit River but still lost. The report in *Power Boating*, however, offered strong praise for Horace's effort and said that *Delphines IV* and *VII* were superb boats that demonstrated great reliability at wide-open speeds. Both boats were built in the Detroit factory and two better race boats would be hard to find anywhere.

Betting on a Recovery

Still, the Horace E. Dodge Boat and Plane Corporation had another surprise up its sleeve for 1934 when it announced the Dodge "Multiple-Vee Double Bottom" at the National Motor Boat Show, explaining the new bottom design as follows:

Each bottom plank laps over the next plank's edge and is fastened through three layers of solid mahogany planking. The

pattern of the laps is the opposite of the traditional lap strake plank arrangement so that each edge provides a lifting force as the hull moves forward and the lifting effect increases with the boats speed. The edges tend to build up water underneath the boat in tracks on which the boat skims along faster that the traditional style bottom surface.

Indications of economic recovery appeared stronger at the 1934 boat show. The boat builders who had held their businesses together and survived the previous four years once more displayed confidence in a brighter future.

Anticipating positive economic news, Dodge again expanded its utility line to include both Standard and Special models in each of four lengths: 16, 19, 20, and 25 feet. The 19-, 20-, and 25-foot models also were offered with optional cabin enclosures.

The expanded utility line, 14 models in all, was a further indication of the growing popularity of the style. What was most significant, however, was that the basic utility was

Always the promoter, Horace Jr. provided buyers with an illustration of Dodge's new bottom design, the "Multiple-Vee Double Bottom" introduced in 1934 to reduce side spray and increase strength and speed through the effect of "tracking and lifting."

In 1935 the 20-foot Special Utility, Model 202-A, was offered with an optional cabin enclosure for an additional $200, thus driving the price up to $1,325 with a 62-horsepower Gray six-cylinder engine. *John Richardson*

The most standard of Standard Utilities was the 1935 Dodge Model 101 16-foot Fishing Boat. At $495 with a 35-horsepower Dodge Brothers four-cylinder engine, it was the lowest-priced boat by a major builder.

called the "Standard" and a more deluxe version was called the "Special."

The development of the Special was a clear signal not only that the utility's style was catching on but that its owners also wanted some luxury features to go with it.

With the addition of deluxe features, plus the wider range of lengths and options for greater overall speed, the utility models became even more popular. The basic painted-hull utilities were still available, but consumer sentiment definitely pointed toward models with nicer features similar to the more attractive runabout models.

Once more, Dodge continued to stay ahead of both Gar Wood and Chris-Craft with its popular utility offerings. Dodge's big

Below: With its natural finish, the 16-foot Fishing Boat was an affordable boat for the average family.
Gary Michael

Dodge's 20-foot Special Cabin Utility came with three engine options and an attractive enclosure featuring a cabin roof that extended further aft to and beyond the windshield to form a practical visor.

25-foot, 3-inch open utility with its 7-foot, 2-inch beam was the first big production utility on the market, a full two years ahead of Chris-Craft's luxurious 24-foot Sportsman. Walt Leveau continued to be the industry's trendsetter, and the new utilities were another example of Dodge's willingness to innovate and to market its products in the midst of the terrible Depression. Horace pointed out in elaborate promotional material a list of Dodge's creative initiatives:

It is no idle boast, but a mere statement of fact that Dodge has consistently led the motor boat industry in the creation, production and introduction of new things in the motor boat field. Beginning with the completion of the largest boat factory in the world in Newport News and starting an entirely new era in motor boat construction using quantity production methods to price boats at unheard of low prices to help popularize boating. Now Dodge has created three new types of all-purpose utility boats to continue to popularize boating.

The Dodge organization demonstrated, once again, its savvy and leadership with the introduction of the utility style.

Boat sales started to make a solid rebound in 1934 and gave hope that the long-awaited economic recovery was under way. Even so, it

Dodge's most advanced utility, the 25-foot, 3-inch Model 502 Special offered in 1934, featured the new Multiple-Vee lapstrake bottom construction, a 7-foot, 2-inch beam, and a top speed of 32 miles per hour, two years ahead of Chris-Craft's 24-foot Sportsman.

remained a nervous time for boat builders as even skeptics started believing that the worst days were over. It would still take most boat builders a few more years to reach the sales levels they achieved back in 1929 prior to the crash.

Wild Cards in the Deck

Dodge prepared its 1935 lineup with two very interesting additions, the first of which surprised nearly everyone: a one-design class, 18-foot sloop-rigged sailboat. Dodge's research showed a new market was developing with one-design sailboats. An association regulated the creation of fixed sailboat designs to encourage competitive racing.

Sailing was particularly popular in the Chesapeake Bay area where the Dodge plant was located, as well as on Long Island Sound. It also was growing rapidly throughout many of the inland lakes regions.

People's economic experiences in the Depression stimulated greater interest in sailing; it was a relatively inexpensive way to enjoy boating and participate in the added pleasures of

competition in organized races involving fleets of similar sailboats. Dodge Boats hoped to capitalize on this rapidly spreading sport by offering its own new sailboat called the Sea Gull for $395.

The other surprise for 1935 was the addition of a standardized 26-foot pocket cruiser. This very attractive cruiser displayed a profile similar to Richardson's popular Little Giant Cruiser models. Dodge gave this compact design a rugged lapstrake hull to provide stiffness and sure handling. The 26-foot cruiser also featured a galley area, a marine toilet compartment, and bunks to sleep four. The small cruiser concept was just beginning to emerge, and this model was attractively priced at $1,995 with a 60-horsepower Gray engine.

The 16-foot runabout, Dodge's all time volume leader, was finally replaced after five years of remarkable popularity. Taking its place in the new 1935 lineup were two totally new 17-foot runabouts. The Model 103 had a double cockpit forward of the engine compartment, while the Model 102 featured a single cockpit forward and another aft of the engine.

The older 25-foot runabout no longer appeared in the Dodge catalog or on the price list and once more was quietly discontinued. The 25-foot, 6-inch runabout was offered both as an open model and with the sedan cabin option with the 165-horsepower Lycoming. The flagship of the Dodge fleet continued to be the 28-foot, 6-inch runabout that was also offered as an attractive landau-style sedan model.

End of an Era

Dodge published a 1936 sales catalog and a 1936 price list but, in reality, ended production by the end of 1935. The end came as somewhat of a surprise for both Dodge's employees and its competition in the boat industry. The most difficult years of the Depression had passed, and those builders who had made it this far were looking at a return to normal times as boat sales climbed steadily to their pre-Depression levels. Yet Horace Dodge's great experiment was abandoned, because the owner and the owner's son had grown tired of the responsibility. Closing the world's largest boat factory after surviving the Depression was an unnecessary blow to Newport News and to the employees who had helped it

Top: Dodge surprised everyone at the 1935 National Motor Boat Show by introducing an attractive 26-foot lapstrake pocket cruiser that could sleep four and sold for less than $2,000.

Above: Horace III and Delphine, children from Horace Jr.'s first marriage to Lois Knowlson, join their father aboard ship to sail to his residence in England in 1935.

endure. Horace's contributions to operating a successful boat business were similar to the effort he put forth in all of his endeavors, whether it was racing, the auto business, or his five marriages, three of which occurred after his grand experiment in boat building. If it was easy, he was ready to take credit, and when it got difficult he was nowhere to be found.

His total lack of commitment to achieving a reasonable goal was a cruel paradox, considering the remarkable dedication that his father had displayed under much more challenging circumstances. In the boat business, Horace was always around for the boat shows, the personal appearances, and the high-profile interviews. But as far as performing the basic tasks of running a successful business were concerned, he didn't measure up in any way.

The key employees of the Dodge boat business did a remarkable job building good

boats for 13 years, from 1923 through 1935, and the company's workers achieved several significant milestones and made lasting contributions that always will be remembered and recognized.

The boat-building activity had not been a profitable experience for the members of the Dodge family, but their losses were still quite manageable in relation to their overall wealth. Horace, however, routinely overstated production estimates in releases to the media. Many of his ideas had merit but were hardly revolutionary. Other boat builders, such as Chris-Craft, perfected practical straight-line production techniques and achieved great success by staying focused on the task at hand. Chris-Craft went on to become the world's largest builder of motorboats after struggling through the Depression years without the vast financial advantages that Dodge possessed.

With any effort on his part, it can be argued that Horace Dodge's success in the boat business would have been virtually guaranteed. The Horace E. Dodge Boat and Plane Corporation was not a victim of the Great Depression. Horace simply decided he was no longer interested, and his mother, who owned the corporation, wasn't going to run it without his participation. The only reason she financed the venture in Virginia was that he agreed to remain in the United States and manage the business, an agreement that he never honored.

One of his marine engine specialists and engineers, Charlie Grafflin, summed up Horace's temperament this way:

Yes, it's too bad Horace wasn't different. He had the pleasure boating business in the palm of his hand. He had the best general manager possible in Bill Horn who was well liked by the entire boating fraternity. My first

The 17-foot split-cockpit Model 102 of 1935 was capable of 35 miles per hour and listed at $1,195. *Matt Dalton*

113

real insight into Horace was when Bill Horn and I won the Gold Cup in 1932 and broke all existing records from the previous twenty years. At the end of the last heat, Bill made another circuit of the course to gradually let the engine cool down and then we headed for

the dock. Bill turned to me and said, "This could cost us our jobs." He was right! Even though we were using one of Horace's old, cast-off hulls and an old engine, Horace resented what we accomplished when he had been trying without success for so long. He never got over it and threw roadblocks in our path from then on.

It is believed that Horace owned more than 30 race boats, although the exact number is unknown. He had more advantages than anybody in racing, yet he always seemed to fall short of expectations. Perhaps the answer was his lack of serious preparation. He had so many boats available for each race that he was rarely committed to the one selected for race day.

Gar Wood, on the other hand, spent endless hours getting to know every detail and every peculiar quirk of his race boats. It was not uncommon for Horace to arrive shortly before the race, having just come from abroad or attended an all-night party.

After discontinuing all standardized boat production in Newport News, Virginia, in 1936, Horace Dodge reopened the facility to build military craft during World War II. Here, Dodge is awarded the coveted Army-Navy "E" on June 22, 1944, for excellent achievements in the production of specialized assault and rescue craft.

Horn's Five Lessons for Success

Bill Horn, who remained with Horace throughout his boat-building years, may have known Horace Dodge better than anyone. He supervised the construction of the new boats at the Newport News factory, was responsible for construction and alterations on Dodge's race boats, and always drove one of the Dodge backup boats in major races. Horn was widely recognized for his personal success as a great driver and was often asked by young drivers seeking advice to share the keys to his success.

Horn's advice was published in *Motor Boating* and summarized in five suggestions: "1. Learn by driving and keep driving as often as possible, 2. Be the master of your boat and become your engine's best friend, 3. Know your boat inside and out and know every quirk of your motor, 4. Prepare for a race with exacting care and thoroughness, and 5. Race cleanly."

If Dodge had followed Horn's approach, he might have been far more successful and even equaled the successes of Gar Wood.

When he opened his boat-building enterprise, Horace was interested primarily in producing race boats for his personal use, just as Gar Wood had done several years before. Neither Wood nor Dodge had to be concerned about developing a profitable boat-building operation because each had an abundance of capital being generated from other sources.

In Wood's case, his money came from his successful hoist business. The notion of building boats for profit was not even a consideration.

Whereas Wood was building very expensive Baby Gar runabouts, Dodge decided that his special niche would be more affordable boats. His concept had a popular ring to it and provided for interesting copy in a variety of periodicals. Other than providing entertaining reading, however, it was never really a serious focus, nor was it achieved.

The Failed Dream

Perhaps the great paradox of Dodge's career was that he developed creative marketing programs and introduced interesting production concepts to an otherwise conservative industry. He also assembled a superior cast of talented associates to help him achieve the goals he envisioned.

Notable achievers such as George Crouch, Walter Leveau, Bill Horn, Earl Hatten, Charlie Grafflin, Martin Draeger, and others all were part of Dodge's organization at one time and provided outstanding contributions to the entire boating industry. Yet marine historians typically refer to the unfortunate closing of Dodge Boats as, simply, another victim of the Great Depression.

In 1923, when Dodge needed a special niche for his new boat enterprise, he adopted the path that had been so successful for Henry Ford. In theory, his approach could make sense, provided boat models were standardized like automobiles and the market was ready to absorb volume production.

With an aggressive approach supported by the Dodge family fortune, he created a national dealership network with the Dodge Brothers Automobile Dealers Association. Such work was very innovative and helped build a substantial following quickly. His program sent a wake-up call to the boating industry that new approaches to building and marketing boats had arrived. By adding designer George Crouch to the Dodge staff, he added even more credibility to his program.

But just as success was within his grasp, Horace let old demons distract him. His immature behavior in 1927 ended six years of marriage and a new love interest drew him out of the country for months at a time. In less than a year, he was married to his second wife and living in England. Crouch, who didn't need the burden of running the entire boat enterprise in Dodge's absence, resigned and returned to New York as an independent designer. Dodge's boat business began to flounder under a cloud of uncertainty regarding its future and total lack of leadership.

When Horace promised to straighten out his life, his mother agreed to finance a giant new boat-building enterprise. Once more, Dodge pledged his complete involvement in the bold new venture with renewed enthusiasm. His new designer, Walter Leveau, prepared a stunning fleet of new models that were the most creative in the industry, while the new company's marketing program established new levels of achievement and drew ever more dealers into the company's program.

When the Depression settled in, Dodge had the unique advantage of great family wealth to

Designed, built, and driven in 1951 by Bill Cantrell for Horace Dodge, the 30-foot *G-31 Hornet* finished second in the 1951 Gold Cup and third in the 1951 President's Cup, shown here.

ride out the difficult times. By 1935 the national recovery was firmly in place and sales began to return to pre-Depression levels. At the same time, the Dodge designers introduced new models for 1935. Suddenly, the Dodge family decided to close the boat business in Newport News.

H.E. Lost in the Bottle

Horace lost interest in building and marketing boats and was spending nearly all his time in England. His drinking had advanced dangerously. His only other interest seemed to be racing. He was just 36 years old, and his focus, such as it was, on meaningful accomplishments was floundering.

One of Horace's former key employees described him this way: "Sober he was a pleasure to be with, pleasant and filled with good ideas; under the influence he was someone we tried to avoid. My impression was that H.E. was an unhappy person and wanted to drown his problems with alcohol. He could have done so much with his boat business and he just threw it away."

Another associate said, "H.E. gets in a race boat once a year for a half an hour or so and thinks he's an expert and that is very frightening! He might run these race boats for a total of three hours a year, himself. The only time he ran them was at the races. Sober, he was smart. He had a good mind and good ideas. But, it was so seldom that he was sober. Drinking he would just do the opposite of what he should be doing just for the hell of it."

Horace always expected to receive his share of the enormous estate created by his father and then controlled by his mother after his father died in 1921. However, both Horace and his sister died before their mother.

Scrounging for Money

Anna Dodge was never confident that either of her children displayed enough financial restraint to be in charge of vast sums of money in the Dodge estate. She may have been correct, but that decision also created an unnatural relationship within the family; Horace and Delphine had a lifelong dependency on their mother for every major financial decision that was required. Legend has it that in 1932 when Horace desperately needed additional funds for race boats, he turned to his sister for help.

He agreed that in return for her gift of $250,000 he would name his race boats *Delphine* in her honor. She agreed and gave him the money from her personal account. Horace honored his commitment to her and named seven race boats *Delphine*, beginning by renaming *Solar Plexus* to *Delphine IV* and continuing through *Delphine X*.

After the sinking of Dodge's original *My Sweetie*, Les Staudacher built a new 30-footer called *My Sweetie Dora*. Equipped with an Allison 1750, she won the 1954 Silver Cup and finished second in the 1956 installment of the race.

My Sweetie wins the 1949 Gold Cup. The boat impressed Horace Dodge so much that he bought her and drove her to a third-place finish in the Harmsworth Trophy Race, attaining an average speed of 81.7 miles per hour. With Bill Cantrell driving for Dodge, she also won the 1949 Silver Cup and the National Sweepstakes. Amazingly, Dodge qualified for the Gold Cup in 1950, 26 years after making his first appearance in the event.

Horace Dodge's ideas, coupled with his family's fortune and the talented people who believed in his plans, produced some of the most exciting boats of the era. Dodge boats represented advanced thinking and cutting-edge technology and designs, and received creative promotional efforts. He boasted that his factory would build 4,000 boats in its first year and more each year following.

John Berryman, former purchasing agent at Dodge's Newport News factory, recalled in a May 20, 1984, interview in the *Newport News Daily Press* that their entire production from 1930 to 1935, for which there are no written records, was 1,600 boats. If his figures were accurate, that would equal an average of 270 boats per year, which may be the reason why surviving examples are so hard to find.

The missing factor was Horace's inability to become the leader of his own enterprises. He was unwilling or, perhaps, unable to do the things that his father and his uncle did to achieve their success. One of the attributes of the Dodge brothers was their ability to perform any operation in their factory with the skill with which they expected their workers to perform. The Dodge brothers were also hard drinkers, but only after their extended workday at the factory was finished.

The Racing Legend

Marine historian William T. Campbell, who specializes in the study of race boats, examined Horace Dodge's racing career along with other important race drivers and reported that Dodge made several great contributions to the sport over a remarkable number of years. He brought a new level of excitement and interest to the Gold Cup races when they needed support the most.

"No one built, developed or entered more boats in Gold Cup Regattas than the Dodges," Campbell wrote. "Horace drove in many races himself including the 1925 Gold Cup, the 1926 Gold Cup and 1922 Sweepstakes. He drove in the 1927 Gold Cup and won the 150-mile Sweepstakes. He set a new displacement record in 1930, drove in the 1933 President's Cup and tried for the Gold Cup mile record in 1937. He drove *Sister Syn* at the 1948 President's Cup and *My Sweetie* in the 1949 Harmsworth and was still driving *My Sweetie* in 1950 at Lake Mead and in 1951 in the Gold Cup race. That's 26 years of racing. Amazing!"

Dodge at War

Six years after Dodge ended its boat production in Newport News, the United States was at war and the government needed a variety of military vessels to patrol our shores. Dodge reopened its factory to build boats for the armed forces. Its production was so exemplary that Dodge was awarded the coveted Army-Navy "E" for excellence in fulfilling its government contracts.

At the conclusion of the war, the Dodge boat factory was offered for sale. In a fitting irony, the successful bidder for the complex that Dodge proclaimed to be "the world's largest

boat factory" was Gar Wood. It was in the former Dodge factory that Gar Wood produced its popular Ensign model utilities. As it turned out, the Gar Wood Ensign built in Newport News, Virginia, at the superb Dodge boat factory, became Gar Wood's biggest seller and its most popular model of all time.

APPENDIX 1

Significant Boat-Building Milestones Attributable to Horace Dodge Jr.'s Standardized Production

1923 – Successfully converted the Dodge Brothers four-cylinder automobile engines to marine use, eventually resulting in Chrysler becoming a major supplier of marine engines; pioneered straight-line boat manufacturing methods.

1924 – Established a national dealer network for servicing Dodge marine engines.

1926 – Standardized the aft-facing rear cockpit seat in his 26-foot Watercar.

1927 – Ran the longest marine advertisement (30 pages) in a single issue of *MotorBoating*; allowed spectators to rotate a 22-foot Watercar from upright to upside down to examine details closely.

1928 – At the National Motor Boat Show displayed a partially planked 26-foot Watercar for spectator examination.

1929 – Placed first full-color marine display ad in a national boating periodical.

1930 – Standardized the first folding V-windshield on production runabouts; standardized twin-windshields on all production runabouts over 20 feet; promoted and sponsored racing for standardized production boats; constructed the world's largest boat factory; introduced the flared boot top on all standardized runabout models.

1932 – The first standardized all-purpose utility model is entered into production; the first standardized cabin utility model is entered into production.

1933 – Incorporated the built-in sun visor styling on cabin utility tops; produced the first production triple-cockpit runabout under 20 feet; developed and patented the Multiple-Vee Bottom construction technique.

1934 – Introduced the first production deluxe utility with the 25-foot, 3-inch model.

1935 – Offered the lowest-priced standardized production inboard at $495; introduced the 18-foot Sea Gull class sailboat into production.

APPENDIX 2

Dodge Standardized Models, 1923 to 1936

The following list is based on research using original Dodge sales brochures, periodical reports, employee correspondence, and Dodge advertising copy. Among this original material, there occur a few instances of inconsistent information. In order to provide information that is believed to be accurate and consistent with the facts available, the author has omitted any recognizable errors. Official model designations established by Dodge are shown in italicized print.

Horace E. Dodge Boat Works, 2670 East Atwater St., Detroit, Michigan
1923

Model	Powerplant	HP	Length	Speed	Price
Yacht Tender		—	15'	—	N/A
Runabout	Dodge-Curtiss	100	20'	35	N/A
Speed Runabout	Liberty	400	33'	45	N/A

(Note: At least one of each type was produced.)

1924

Model	Powerplant	HP	Length	Speed	Price
Watercar Long-Deck Runabout	Dodge	30	22' 2"	20	$2,475

(Note: The first 111 22-foot Watercars were subcontracted to the Racine Manufacturing Company in Racine, Wisconsin, in 1924, with Martin Draeger appointed project supervisor before the Dodge factory went into production.)

1925

Model	Powerplant	HP	Length	Speed	Price
Watercar Long-Deck Runabout	Dodge	30	22' 2"	20	$2,475

Horace E. Dodge Boat Works, 554-616 Lycaste Avenue, Detroit, Michigan
1926

Model	Powerplant	HP	Length	Speed	Price
Model 422 Watercar Long-Deck Runabout	Dodge	30	22' 6"	20	$2,475
Model 822 Watercar Long-Deck Runabout	Dodge-Curtiss	90	22' 6"	35	$2,975
Model 826 Watercar Triple-Cockpit Runabout	Dodge-Curtiss	90	26' 6"	33	$3,475
Model 630 Watercar Senior Triple-Cockpit Runabout	Globe	250	30'	45	$7,200

1927

Model	Powerplant	HP	Length	Speed	Price
Model 422 Watercar Long-Deck Runabout	Dodge	30–35	26' 6"	20	$2,195
Model 822 Watercar Long-Deck Runabout	Dodge-Curtiss	100	22' 6"	37	$2,765
Model 826 Watercar Triple-Cockpit Runabout (9–12 passenger)	Dodge-Curtiss	100	26'	35	$3,265

Model	Powerplant	HP	Length	Speed	Price
Model 630 Watercar Senior Triple-Cockpit Runabout	Globe	250	30'	45	$7,200

1928

Model	Powerplant	HP	Length	Speed	Price
Sport-A-Bout Runabout	Dodge	35	20'	25	$1,595
Runabout	Dodge-Curtiss	100	26'	33	$3,265
Runabout	Globe or Hall-Scott	250/200	30'	45	$7,800

1929

Model	Powerplant	HP	Length	Speed	Price
Runabout	Dodge	35	20'	22–25	$1,675
Runabout	6-cylinder		20'	30	$2,100
Watercar Long-Deck Runabout	Dodge/Dodge-Curtiss	35/100	22' 6"	24/37	$3,265
Watercar Runabout	Lycoming	115	26'	33-35	$3,265
Watercar Senior Runabout	Hall-Scott	200	30'	40	$7,200

The Horace E. Dodge Boat and Plane Corp., 1300 Marshall Ave., Newport News, Virginia

1930

Model	Powerplant	HP	Length	Speed	Price
Runabout	Lycoming	40	16'	25	$945
Runabout	Lycoming	115	21'	35	$2,100
Model 3 Runabout	Lycoming	125	25'	32	$2,500
Model 4 Runabout	Lycoming	165	25'	38	$3,200
Model 10 Sedan	Lycoming	165	25'	34	$3,900
Model 5 Runabout	Lycoming	165	28'	32	$3,700
Model 6 Runabout	Lycoming	300	28'	45	$4,500
Model 11 Sedan	Lycoming	300	28'	38	$5,300
Double Cabin Express Cruiser	Lycoming	2x300	45'	35	$27,500

1931

Model	Powerplant	HP	Length	Speed	Price
Runabout	Lycoming	40	16'	30	$1,095
Runabout	Lycoming	125	21' 6"	35	$2,295
Model 3 Runabout	Lycoming	125	25'	32	$2,595
Model 4 Runabout	Lycoming	165	25'	35	$3,195
Model 10 Sedan	Lycoming	165	25'	34	$3,895
Special Runabout	Lycoming	300	25' 6"	47	$4,795
Model 5 Runabout	Lycoming	165	28'	34	$4,500
Model 6 Runabout	Lycoming	325	28'	46	$5,795
Model 5-S Sedan	Lycoming	165	28'	32	$5,300
Model 11 Sedan	Lycoming	325	28'	43	$5,795

1932

Model	Powerplant	HP	Length	Speed	Price
Model 201 Runabout	Lycoming	45	16' 3"	30	$840
Model 203 Special Utility	Lycoming	45	19'	18	$795
Model 202 Utility (painted hull)	Lycoming	45	19'	18	$695
Cabin Utility	Lycoming	66	19'	22	$1,095
Cabin Utility	Lycoming	45	19'	16	$795
Model 204 Runabout	Lycoming	90	19' 5"	34	$1,385
Model 205-A Runabout	Lycoming	115	19' 5"	36	$1,745
Model 206 Runabout	Lycoming	90	23' 5"	37	$1,995
Model 207 Runabout	Lycoming	125	23' 5"	34	$2,295

Model	Powerplant	HP	Length	Speed	Price
Model 208 Runabout	Lycoming	165	25' 6"	37	$3,195
Model 208-S Sedan	Lycoming	165	25' 6"	33	$3,995
Model 209 Runabout	Lycoming	325	25' 6"	48	$5,495
Custom Model 210 Runabout	Lycoming	165	28' 7"	34	$3,695
Model 210-S Sedan	Lycoming	165	28' 7"	32	$4,495
Custom Model 211 Runabout	Lycoming	325	28' 7"	46	$5,795
Custom Model 211-S Sedan	Lycoming	325	28' 7"	43	$6,895

1933

Model	Powerplant	HP	Length	Speed	Price
Model 301 Utility	Lycoming	45	16'	25	$545
Model 201 Runabout	Lycoming	45	16' 3"	30	$795
Model 202-G Utility	Lycoming	66	19'	24	$995
Model 202 Utility	Lycoming	45	19'	18	$695
Model 202-GK Cabin Utility	Lycoming	66	19'	22	$1,095
Model 203 Cabin Utility	Lycoming	45	19'	18	$795
Model 204 Runabout	Lycoming	90	19' 5"	34	$1,385
Model 207 Runabout	Lycoming	115	25'	32	$1,995
Model 208 Runabout	Lycoming	165	25' 6"	37	$3,195
Model 208-S Sedan	Lycoming	165	25' 6"	33	$3,995
Model 210 Runabout	Lycoming	165	28' 7"	34	$3,695
Model 210-S Sedan	Lycoming	165	28' 7"	32	$4,495
Model 211 Runabout	Lycoming	325	28' 7"	46	$5,795
Model 211-S Sedan	Lycoming	325	28' 7"	43	$6,895

1934

Model	Powerplant	HP	Length	Speed	Price
Model 301 Standard Utility	Lycoming	45	16'	25	$595
Model 301 Special Utility	Lycoming	45	16'	29	$695
Model 201 Runabout	Lycoming	45	16' 3"	30	$695
Model 202 Standard Utility	Lycoming	45	19'	18	$695
Model 202-A Standard Cabin Utility	Lycoming	62	19'	25	$845
Model 204 Runabout	Gray	93	19' 5"	34	$1,385
Model 402 Special Utility	Lycoming	45	20'	24	$895
Model 402-A Special Utility	Gray	62	20'	25	$1,045
Model 402-B Special Utility	Gray	93	20'	32	$1,145
Model 207 Runabout	Lycoming	115	25'	32	$1,995
Model 502 Special Utility	Lycoming	115	25' 3"	32	$2,195
Model 502-A Special Utility	Lycoming	165	25' 3"	35	$2,595
Model 208 Runabout	Lycoming	165	25' 6"	35	$3,195
Model 208-S Sedan	Lycoming	165	25' 6"	33	$3,995
Model 210 Runabout	Lycoming	165	28' 7"	34	$3,695
Model 210-S Sedan	Lycoming	169	28' 7"	32	$4,495
Model 211 Runabout	Lycoming	325	28' 7"	47	$5,795
Model 211-S Sedan	Lycoming	325	28' 7"	45	$6,895

1935

Model	Powerplant	HP	Length	Speed	Price
Model 101 Standard Utility Fishing Boat	Dodge	35	16'	25	$495
Model 301 Standard Utility	Lycoming	45	16'	25	$650
Model 302 Special Utility	Lycoming	45	16'	25	$755
Model 103 Runabout Double Cockpit Forward	Gray	60	17'	32	$945

Model	Powerplant	HP	Length	Speed	Price
Model 102 Runabout Cockpits Fore and Aft	Gray	80	17'	35	$1,195
Model 102-A Runabout Cockpits Fore and Aft	Gray	115	17'	40	$1,395
Model 104 Runabout Double Cockpit Forward	Gray	97	19' 5"	36	$1,485
Model 401 Standard Utility	Lycoming	45	20'	22	$975
Model 401-A Standard Utility	Gray	62	20'	25	$975
Model 401-B Standard Utility	Gray	97	20'	28	$1,075
Model 402 Special Utility	Lycoming	45	20'	24	$975
Model 402-A Special Utility	Gray	62	20'	28	$1,125
Model 402-B Special Utility	Gray	97	20'	32	$1, 225
Model 208 Runabout	Lycoming	165	25' 6"	35	$3,395
Model 208-S Sedan	Lycoming	165	25' 6"	33	$4,195
Model 210 Runabout	Lycoming	165	28' 6"	34	$3,845
Model 210-S Sedan	Lycoming	165	28' 6"	32	$4,645
Model 211 Runabout	Lycoming	325	28' 6"	47	$5,795
Model 211-S Sedan	Lycoming	325	28' 6"	45	$6,895
Model 50 Cruiser	Gray	80	26'	18	$2,195
Model 50-A Cruiser	Gray	60	26'	14	$1,995
Model 25 Sea Gull Sailboat	Sail Area 165 sq. ft.	—	18'	—	$395

(Note: A cabin enclosure was available on Models 401, 401-A, 401-B, 402, 402-A, and 402-B for an additional $200.)

1936

Model	Powerplant	HP	Length	Speed	Price
Model 101 Special Fisherman's Boat	Dodge	35	16'	24	$565
Model 302 Deluxe Utility	Lycoming	45	16'	26	$795
Model 103 Family Runabout	Gray	60	17'	29	$945
Model 102 Runabout	Lycoming	96	17'	35	$1,195
Model 102-A Runabout	Lycoming	115	17'	40	$1,395
Model 104 Runabout	Gray	97	19' 5"	33	$1,495
Model 402 Deluxe Utility	Lycoming	45	20'	18	$975
Model 402-A Deluxe Utility	Lycoming	96	20'	28	$1,125
Model 208 Runabout	Lycoming	165	25' 6"	34	$3,395
Model 208-S Sedan	Lycoming	165	25' 6"	32	$4,195
Model 211 Runabout	Lycoming	325	28' 6"	47	$5,795
Model 211-S Sedan	Lycoming	325	28' 6"	43	$6,895
Model 210 Runabout	Lycoming	165	28' 6"	32	$3,845
Model 210-S Sedan	Lycoming	165	28' 6"	30	$4,645
Model 50 Cruiser	Lycoming	96	26'	17	$2,295
Model 50-A Cruiser	Gray	60	26'	12	$2,095
Model 25 Sea Gull Sailboat	Sail Area 165 sq. ft.	—	18'	—	$395

(Note: A cabin enclosure was available on Models 402 and 402-A for an additional $200.)

APPENDIX 3

Important Dodge Race Boats

The following list of Dodge race boats includes selected examples that were built for, or acquired by, the Dodge family. The Dodges owned many race boats, some of which are not listed here. Dodge race boats often were modified or provided with frequent engine changes. In some cases, the boats were renamed while still in Dodge ownership. This list has been prepared from various original articles and racing reports and is believed to be as accurate as the sources from which it was prepared.

The letters preceding the racing numbers indicate the following: **T**=Sweepstakes, **U**=Unlimited, **G**=Gold Cup, **D**=Development Class

1922 – *Baby Holo*, S-32: 20-footer designed by Bill Crowley, built by Belle Isle Boat Company, and powered with a Liberty engine. Established a new world speed record of 64.1 mph in the 2,200ci hydroplane class for a single lap in the 1922 International Great Lakes Championship Trophy Race in Buffalo, New York, with Bill "Oregon Kid" Crowley driving.

1923 – *Musketeer I*, T-40: 27-footer turned over in the trial run for the 1923 Sweepstakes with Bill Horn driving. Won the 1923 International Great Lakes Gold Cup Challenge Trophy with Horace Dodge driving in a field of "nine of the fastest displacement boats in the country."

1924 – *Baby Horace III*, T-46: 24-footer designed by George Crouch and powered by a 12-cylinder Packard Sweepstakes engine Finished sixth in the 1924 150-Mile Sweepstakes Race with W. Abar driving. Finished just 12 seconds behind the winner (*Packard Chriscraft II*, driven by Col. Jesse Vincent) in the 1925 Sweepstakes with Caleb Bragg driving. Horace Dodge drove his boat to a one-mile speed record of 60.3 mph for displacement runabouts. ***Baby Horace III*** is fully restored and currently in private ownership.

1925 – *Solar Plexus*, G-31: 25 feet, 5 inches long by 6 feet wide, this George Crouch design was Packard-powered, built by the Horace Dodge Boat Works, and driven in the 1925 Gold Cup by Horace Dodge. It withdrew during the first and second laps and did not start in the final heat. Finished sixth in the 1926 Gold Cup with Bill Horn driving, finished sixth in the President's Cup, and won the 1927 Detroit Yacht Club Development Class Race with F. G. Ericson driving. Ericson finished second in-150-Mile Sweepstakes behind Horace Dodge who was driving ***Miss Syndicate***. *Solar Plexus* was renamed ***Delphine IV*** in 1931 and provided with a new shingled bottom completed at the Dodge Newport News factory under the direction of Bill Horn. Won the 1932 Gold Cup Trophy and the 1932 President's Cup with Bill Horn driving. Finished second in 1933 and second in the 1934 Gold Cup Races. In 1979 Bill Morgan built a superb replica of ***Delphine IV*** that remains in private ownership.

1925 – *Impshi*, G-36: 27 feet, 9 inches by 6 feet wide, *Impshi* was another Packard-powered George Crouch design. It was driven by William Joyce to a fourth-place finish in the 1925 Gold Cup at the Columbia Yacht Club in New York. Dodge drove *Impshi* to fourth place in the 1926 Gold Cup. The bottom was shingled and the boat returned to competition as ***Delphine VI*** in 1932. In 1933 it was driven by F. G. Ericson with a Dodge-Miller engine in the Gold Cup but dropped out during the first heat after running "a good second." Sold to John Shibe and renamed ***Ethyl Ruth III***. Purchased again by Dodge and raced in Palm Beach against Count Rossi's Italian team. Purchased by Aaron DeRoy and raced as ***Hornet*** in the 1934 Gold Cup and President's Cup races. Repurchased by Dodge and renamed ***Impshi***. Entered the 1935 Gold Cup, but a broken connecting rod kept it from starting the race. Repowered with a new Packard engine, it won the 1936 Gold Cup for Dodge with Kaye Don driving when the defending champion, *El Lagarto*, lasted less than one minute in the final heat. In the 1937 Gold Cup Race its gearbox "went to pieces." At least two replicas have been built and are in private ownership.

1925 – *Nuisance*, G-9: 27-foot, 9-inch by 6-foot George Crouch design with a Packard Gold Cup Special engine was entered in the 1925 Gold Cup by Delphine Dodge Cromwell and driven by Col. Jesse Vincent. Won the first heat but was forced to withdraw with a broken shaft in the second. Won the 1925 Detroit Yacht Club Challenge Cup. Driven by Mrs. Cromwell in the 1925 150-Mile Sweepstakes until forced out with a broken shaft after completing 102 miles. Horace entered ***Nuisance*** in the 1927 Gold Cup Race but was forced to withdraw with motor trouble. Purchased and raced by Jack Dunn as ***Jay-Dee*** and in 1941 as ***Miss Miami Beach***.

1925 – *Miss Syndicate*, D-1: 34 feet, 8 inches long by 6 feet, 6 inches wide, this George Crouch design was, powered by a Dodge-Liberty engine of 450 horsepower. Built for the Dodge Brothers Dealers Association, which sponsored the boat. In second place after 147 miles in the 1926 150-Mile Sweepstakes, Dodge was forced out by a mechanical failure. It won the 1927 150-Mile National Sweepstakes with Horace Dodge driving at an average speed 47.5 mph and a best average lap speed of 54 mph. Won the 1927 President's Cup with Horace driving the first two heats and his sister, Delphine, driving the third. Tied for second in the 1940 Gold Cup and tied for third in the 1940 President's Cup.

1926 – *Watercar Detroit*: Stock 26-foot Watercar runabout hull with Packard Gold Cup 6-cylinder engine, driven by James Cromwell (Delphine's husband) in the 1926 Sweepstakes and the 1926 Gold Cup.

1926 – *Baby Watercar*, G-34: Reportedly based on a 26-foot, 6-inch standardized Watercar runabout Model 826 hull. Powered with a 24-cylinder Duesenberg of 420–440 horsepower and renamed ***Bottoms Up*** in 1927. ***Baby Watercar*** is in the permanent exhibit at the Antique Boat Museum in Clayton, New York.

1926 – *Horace*, D-37: 37 feet, 2 inches long by 7 feet, 8 inches wide, this George Crouch design with a 650-horsepower, 12-cylinder Wright-Typhoon engine was owned by Mrs. Anna Dodge Dillman. Won the 1926 Potomac River Championship Race, finished second in the third heat of the 1926 President's Cup, and started the 1926 150-Mile Sweepstakes but dropped out in the eleventh lap. Now resides in a West Coast auto museum.

1927 – *Sister Syn*, T-30: 32-foot George Crouch design with Packard Sweepstakes power raced by Delphine Dodge Cromwell. Took third place in the 1927 President's Cup. Repowered with an Allison by Horace Dodge in 1948 in preparation for the Gold Cup and the President's Cup. Has been restored and is in private ownership.

1931 – *Miss Syndicate* III, G-15: Designed by Fred Cooper and built in Newport News, Virginia. A single-step hydroplane with 24-cylinder Duesenberg rear-mounted engine, was driven by Dodge in the 1932 Gold Cup Race but was forced out of the first heat when the engine lost oil pressure. Driven by Dodge in the 1932 President's Cup Race. Repowered with a supercharged Packard V-12 (550 horsepower) and renamed ***Delphine V*** in 1932 and entered in 1933 Harmsworth defense with two of Gar Wood's *Miss Americas*. A backfire before the first race started a fire that destroyed the boat.

1931 – *Delphine IV*, G-31 (see 1925)

1932 – *Delphine V*, G-15 (see 1931)

1933 – *Delphine VI*, G-36 (see 1925)

1933 – *Delphine VII*, G-37: George Crouch design owned by Delphine Dodge Baker was of unusual construction with battens on the outside of the hull—appears to be lapstrake but is not. Built in the Newport News factory. Owned by Delphine Dodge Baker and driven by her to third place in the 1933 Gold Cup. Driven by Dodge in the 1933 Virginia Gold Cup and Dodge Memorial Trophy victories. Placed second in the 1933 President's Cup and Gold Cup.

1933 – *Delphine IX*, G-39: Cooper design built in England with 12-cylinder rear-mounted engine. Ran poorly in 1933 Gold Cup Race. Refitted with a V-16 Miller engine and set a single-lap record of 67.5 mph in the 1937 Gold Cup but failed to finish the second and third heats. Did not start after the first heat of the 1937 President's Cup. Did not start for the first heat of 1938 Gold Cup Race.

1936 – *Impshi*, G-36 (see 1925)

1938 – *Excuse Me*, G-2: 24-foot Fred Cooper design with Packard Gold Cup power disintegrated in the 1938 Gold Cup with Bill Horn driving.

1948 – *My Sweetie*, G-3, U-3: Purchased by Dodge after it won the 1949 Gold Cup Regatta. 30 feet, 8 inches long by 8 feet wide, a John Hacker design with a 12-cylinder, 1,500-horsepower Allison engine. Dodge drove it to third in the Harmsworth Trophy Race at an average speed of 81.7 mph. Won the 1949 Silver Cup. Won the 1949 National Sweepstakes with Bill Cantrell driving. Finished third in the 1950 Gold Cup. Amazingly, Dodge himself qualified for the 1951 Gold Cup averaging 72 mph 26 years after his first Gold Cup appearance. Altogether won seven races in 1949. Flipped and sank in the 1956 Silver Cup. Dodge added three more ***My Sweeties***, including: **1954 – *My Sweetie Dora*, U-14**, 30 feet, 3 inches long, Staudacher-built, Allison 1,750ci winner of the 1954 Silver Cup, second in 1956 with Jack Barlow driving; **1954 – *Little My Sweetie***, finished second in 1954 Silver Cup, John Ban driving; and **1954 – *My Sweetie John Francis*, U-17**, Staudacher-built, 1,750ci Allison.

1951 – *Hornet*, G-31: 30 feet long by 12 feet, 4 inches wide, this three-point hull designed and built by Bill Cantrell finished second in the 1951 Gold Cup and third in the President's Cup with Cantrell driving.

BIBLIOGRAPHY

Ballantyne, Philip B. *Classic American Runabouts*. Osceola, WI: MBI Publishing Company, 2001.

Campbell, Jr., William T. *Speedboat Scrapbook*. Vol. 2. Downington, PA: 1992.

———. *Speedboat Scrapbook*. Vol. 3. Downington, PA: 1998.

Dodge, Jr., Horace E. "Mass Production for Boats." *Motor Boating* February 1930: 106–7, 169, 184.

Draeger, Martin. "Build or Manufacture." *Boating* December 1924: 10–11.

———. "Hull Production." *Rudder* 1925: 16-19.

Edenburn, W. D. "Dodge Sponsors Six in Sweepstakes." *The Main Sheet*, Detroit Yacht Club, vol. 12, no. 8 (August 1925).

Fostle, D. W. *Speedboat*. Mystic, CT: United States Historical Society & Mystic Seaport Museum, 1988.

Guetat, Gerald. *Classic Speedboats, 1916–1939*. Osceola, WI: Motorbooks International, 1997.

Haversack, The. Yearbook of the Manlius Military Academy, 1918, 1919, and 1920.

"Horace, a 58-Mile Yacht Tender." *Motor Boat* 10 December, 1926: 10.

Kofoed, V. Beckwith. "How Boats Are Manufactured Today." *Motor Boating* January 1931: 128–31, 226, 228.

Latham, Caroline, and David Agresta. *Dodge Dynasty: The Car and the Family That Rocked Detroit*. New York: Harcourt Brace Jovanovich, 1989.

Lowell, Ben. "Elgin." *Classic Boating* July/August 1997: 28–31.

McPherson, Thomas A. *The Dodge Story*. Osceola, WI: Motorbooks International, 1975.

Morris, Everett B. "Delphine IV Wins Gold Cup." *New York Herald Tribune* 4 September 1933.

Pitrone, Jean Maddern. *Tangled Web: Legacy of Auto Pioneer John F. Dodge*. Hamtramck, MI: Avenue Publishing, 1989.

Pitrone, Jean Maddern, and Joan Potter Elwart. *The Dodges: The Auto Family Fortune and Misfortune*. South Bend, IN: Icarus Press, 1981.

Rouse, Parke. "Wealthy Horace E. Dodge." *Newport News Daily Press* 20 May 1984, sec. C3.

Speltz, Robert G. *The Real Runabouts II*. Lake Mills, IA: Graphic Publishing Company, 1986.

Sutton, Jr., George W. "Why We Are Leading a Boat Revolution." *Motor Boating* February 1927: 79-84.

True, Frank C. "More Boats in Use This Year." *The New York Sun* February 1932.

"Watercars Improved." *Motor Boating* November 1925: 33, 140.

INDEX